Warnock's Eighteen l

Warnock's Eighteen Per Cent

*Children with Special Needs
in Primary Schools*

*Caroline Gipps, Harriet Gross
and Harvey Goldstein*

 The Falmer Press

(A member of the Taylor and Francis Group)
London, New York and Philadelphia

UK   The Falmer Press, Falmer House, Barcombe, Lewes, East Sussex, BN8 5DL

USA   The Falmer Press, Taylor & Francis Inc., 242 Cherry Street, Philadelphia, PA 19106-1906

First published 1987

Library of Congress Cataloging in Publication Data

Gipps, C. V.
  Warnock's eighteen per cent.

  1. Remedial teaching. 2. Handicapped children—
Education—Great Britain. I. Gross, Harriet (Harriet M.)
II. Goldstein, Harvey. III. Title. IV. Title:
Warnock's 18%.
LB1029.R4G54 1986 371.9 86-29348
ISBN 1-85000-139-1
ISBN 1-85000-140-5 (pbk.)

Jacket design by Caroline Archer

Typeset in 11/13 Bembo by
Imago Publishing Ltd, Thame, Oxon

Printed in Great Britain by Taylor & Francis (Printers) Ltd, Basingstoke

Contents

Acknowledgements		vi
List of Tables and Figures		vii
Glossary		ix
Introduction		xi
1	From Remedial Teaching to Special Needs Provision	1
2	Screening and Identification	15
3	How LEAs and Teachers Identify Children with Special Needs	24
4	Provision for Children with Special Needs	35
5	The Case Studies: Six LEAs	48
6	The Teachers	65
7	Implications of the Teachers' Feelings	83
8	The Children	91
9	Conclusions	120
References		136
Index		141

Acknowledgements

The research study on which this report is based was funded by the Economic and Social Research Council whose support is gratefully acknowledged. However, the views expressed in this report are not necessarily those of the ESRC.

We should like to thank our Advisory Group: Professor K. Wedell (Chairperson), Professor G. Bernbaum, Dr T. Blackstone, Mr K. Cornwall (until 1985), Dr S. Hegarty, Dr G. Lindsay (from April 1985), Mr C. Marshall and Dr J. Welton. Their advice was always timely and supportive. We thank the two project secretaries, Jenny Read and Ann Aitken who unflinchingly typed and retyped, processed and reprocessed our questionnaires, letters and manuscripts.

Finally, our thanks and regards must go to the six LEAs and thirty schools which opened their doors to us and let us ask, probe, discuss and observe with great patience. It is easy for us to say, with hindsight, how they might have organized things differently. May we just say that in every LEA we were impressed by the level of commitment to children with special needs and we hope this comes through in the pages which follow.

List of Tables and Figures

Tables

1	Percentage of children with SN at ages 7 and 11	19
2	Screening programmes by type of LEA	24
3	Number of LEAs having one or more screening programmes	25
4	Ages at which screening occurs	25
5	Types of test used in screening programmes	26
6	Reading tests used in LEAs screening	26
7	Year of introduction of screening programmes	27
8	How teachers identify children with special needs	32
9	Teachers' use of test scores in screening and non-screening LEAs	32
10	How teachers identify children as needing outside help	33
11	Number of PRT/RAT/SN support staff in LEAs	41
12	Number of PRT/RAT/SN support staff by size of LEA	42
13	Staffing changes in the last five years	42
14	Availability of provision	43
15	Background details of the sample of teachers	66
16	In-service training by LEA	67
17	Class sizes in schools visited	67
18	Percentage of children with special needs in class	68
19	The best way to help children with SN: Norborough teachers' rank ordering	70
20	Teacher satisfaction in Norborough	70
21	The best way to help children with SN: Southshire teachers' rank ordering	72
22	Teacher satisfaction in Southshire	72
23	The best way to help children with SN: Suburb teachers' rank ordering	73
24	Teacher satisfaction in Suburb	74

25	The best way to help children with SN: Ruralshire teachers' rank ordering	75
26	Teacher satisfaction in Ruralshire	76
27	The best way to help children with SN: Newtown teachers' rank ordering	77
28	Teacher satisfaction in Newtown	77
29	The best way to help children with SN: Midshire teachers' rank ordering	79
30	Teacher satisfaction in Midshire	79
31	Teacher satisfaction — all teachers	80
32	The best way to help children with SN: All teachers	80
33	Average rankings in order of preference	81
34	The children: Basic information	93

Figures

1	The hits and misses evaluation model	19
2	Names of support services	40

Glossary

ACO	Area Coordinator
BPS	British Psychological Society
BSC	Basic Skills Checklist
BSSS/T	Basic Skills Support Service/Team
CDT	Craft Design and Technology
DES	Department of Education and Science
EP	Educational Psychologist
ESN(M)	Educationally Subnormal (Moderate)
FTE	Full-time equivalent
HMI	Her Majesty's Inspectorate
JM&I	Junior, mixed and infants
LDSS	Learning Difficulties Support Service
LDT	Learning Difficulties Tutors
LEA	Local Education Authority
NARE	National Association for Remedial Education
NAS/UWT	National Association of Schoolmasters/Union of Women Teachers
NUT	National Union of Teachers
OTIS	One Term In-service Course
PEP	Principal Educational Psychologist
PRT	Peripatetic Remedial Teacher
PTR	Pupil/Teacher Ratio
RAT	Remedial Advisory Teacher
RC	Remedial Centre
RQ	Reading Quotient
SEN	Special Educational Needs
SN	Special Needs
SNAP	Special Needs Action Programme
SNC	Special Needs Coordinator

Glossary

SNS	Special Needs Service
SNST	Special Needs Support Team
SPS	Schools Psychological Service
TES	Times Educational Supplement

Introduction

This book is about how children who need special help in school are identified and how such help is given to them. It reports the findings of a three-year research project on screening and special educational provision.[1]

Remedial teaching has long been part of primary school life, usually a fairly low status activity, with remedial children withdrawn from their classrooms by a visiting or part-time teacher. In the late 1970s, however, something happened to change all this. The remedial child became the child with special needs, and remedial education became a higher status activity, with money found for in-service training and new posts. This highly skilled professional task was now to be seen first and foremost as the responsibility of the class teacher, perhaps helped by a support service, the same class teacher who in the past had usually been encouraged to pass these children on to someone else for intervention.

Special needs has been a growth area in education for almost ten years now. The major emphasis, however, has been on the assessment of (statementing) and provision for (whether and how to integrate) children with quite severe difficulties in either physical, emotional or intellectual development. That is, the so-called '2 per cent' who pre-1978 would most probably have been educated in separate special schools and units. Less attention has been given to those children with special needs who, while having difficulties at school, would never have been considered for a special school or unit. This is a much larger group of children, typically considered to be in the region of 18 per cent of the school population.

The emphasis on the needs of the smaller group of children with quite severe difficulties emanated from growing social and ideological demands for a fairer deal for this minority group. The implementation and monitoring of the special education integration movement has, however, tended to overshadow the fate of the greater number of children who have special needs but are in ordinary schools. Far less attention, certainly in research terms, has been paid to what is happening to the child who was once described as 'remedial'.

The changes in 'remedial' education over the last ten years have happened in a relatively uncharted way, with apparently great variation from one LEA to another, and we felt that the developments had potentially serious implications for teachers and children. One of our reasons for carrying out the study was, therefore, to monitor these changes and to try and assess their impact on schools and children. In addition, since in order to provide help for children, they must first be identified, and this is part of the LEA's duty, we were also concerned to investigate this aspect of the process. Our own· previous research had shown that many LEAs had testing programmes which they called 'screening' programmes but these apparently played only a small part in the school level identification of children with special needs (Gipps *et al*, 1983).

How We Did the Study

Our aim was to look at policy and practice in identification of, and provision for, children with special needs in the primary school. Because the term special needs covers such a range of children, we restricted our focus to primary aged children with learning difficulties in the basic skills, at a level which would normally be catered for within the ordinary school.

We were interested in policy and practice at every level from LEA to child via the school. We therefore started with the LEA and moved our focus progressively towards schools and classrooms.[2] First, we sent a questionnaire to every LEA in England and Wales asking about their policies for identification and provision for children with special needs. Questions included whether they had a screening/identification programme, about their remedial/special needs support service, and about any changes in policy or staffing in this area over the previous five years. The findings from this questionnaire, relating to policy at LEA level over the country as a whole, are reported in chapters 3 and 4.

On the basis of these questionnaire results and interviews with LEA staff in ten local authorities we identified six LEAs as case study areas.

The six case study LEAs were carefully selected to cover a range of type of LEA, geographical area, presence/absence of a screening programme and type of support service. These six LEAs are described briefly in chapter 5.

In the case study LEAs we interviewed those individuals who were most significant in the control and running of the support service, or in the case of one LEA where there was no support service, the Schools Psychological Service. The interviews generally involved at least the principal educational psychologist, adviser for special needs, assistant education officer (special needs) and heads of remedial/support services. These semi-structured interviews were designed to find out more about LEAs' policies than was possible in a questionnaire, together with the impact of the cuts and the 1981 Act, and specifically the political, historical, economic and geographical reasons for having the policies which they had. The detailed descriptions which resulted from these interviews form the basis of the companion volume to this (*Supporting Warnock's Eighteen Per Cent*, Gross and Gipps) but the data serve to inform the rest of this book, in particular chapter 9.

Finally, five schools were chosen in each of the six LEAs. These were primary schools (in the case of one LEA first and middle schools) selected by the LEA to represent in their view a broad range of interest in, and take up of, special needs support. Of course we were not aware at the time of our visits which schools the LEA considered to be at which end of the continuum.

Three day visits were made to each of the schools during which time the researchers interviewed the head and any visiting educational psychologist or support/remedial staff. Every class teacher was given a short questionnaire and informal discussions were held in the staffrooms over the three days. The teachers' views about LEA policy and how it was working in practice in their classrooms form the material for chapters 6 and 7.

Within each school we focussed on one classroom and within that class two children identified as being fairly typical special needs children. We had extended discussions with the class teachers about these children: how they were identified, what extra help there was for them, whether their curriculum differed from the rest of the class and so on. We looked at the children's records for as far back as they were available to get their histories. Finally we observed them in a semi-structured way over two half days, including whenever possible any special help they received whether in or out of the classroom, and in or out of school. What the different LEA policies mean for the children is described in chapter 8.

The issues in which we were particularly interested were:

— the usefulness of screening programmes;
— the impact of changes in support services on teachers and children;
— managing these changes;
— the impact of the cuts in educational expenditure and the 1981 Act on central and school-based provision;
— withdrawal teaching versus other models of support.

We deal with each of these issues in the next eight chapters as they become relevant, and in chapter 9 we draw together the main conclusions, relating them to the issues outlined above. Finally we look forward and identify the features that will concern LEAs or schools which may be considering changes. For example, whether screening is useful in all LEAs; the problems in using packages developed in other LEAs; how new support services might be put over to teachers and how liaison might be improved to increase the value of support to children.

We now turn to chapter 1 and set the study in its historical and educational perspective.

Notes

1 This project was funded by the Economic and Social Research Council at the Institute of Education, University of London, from 1983 to 1986.
2 Copies of the questionnaires and interview schedules used, and details of the observation method are available from the authors at the Institute of Education, Bedford Way, London WC1H OAL (Screening and Special Educational Provision in Schools Project final report to ESRC, April 1986).

Chapter 1

From Remedial Teaching to Special Needs Provision

In the Introduction we referred to changes that took place in remedial education in the late 1970s and early 1980s. In this chapter we set the scene by describing these changes in more detail and outlining some of the reasons for the changes. We consider the origin of the term 'special needs' and where the figures of 2 per cent and 18 per cent come from.

The Changing Face of Remedial Education

What were the changes that came about in remedial education and why did they happen? We need first to look at 'why' because that makes it easier to understand the form that these changes took. Three key things precipitated the radical rethinking of the role of remedial education. One was a concern about the lack of medium and long-term effectiveness of traditional remedial teaching methods, another was the impact of the cuts in local authority expenditure on levels of remedial staffing and the third was the Warnock Report.

The Warnock Report

In 1978 the Warnock Report on Special Educational Needs suggested that special needs should be viewed as a continuum, and that special education be seen as encompassing the whole range and variety of additional means by which children may be helped to overcome educational difficulties. Both remedial education and special education were to be drawn into the definition:

At present 'remedial' groups include children with a variety of difficulties which, though different in origin, are frequently treated alike.... The term 'remedial', like the term 'treatment', suggests that these children have something wrong with them that can be put right. It is true that some of them are suffering only a temporary learning difficulty ... Others, however, require special help and support throughout their school lives and to say that these children require 'remedial' education is misleading. ... For these children the provision of special support is just as important as for those who have been ascertained as requiring special education. *We conclude that a meaningful distinction between remedial and special education can no longer be maintained.* (DES, 1978a, para 3.39, p. 47, our emphasis)

Thus the remedial child became the child with special needs. Although this equates remedial with special needs, the relationship is not reciprocal; the remedial child is a child with special needs but a child with special needs may not have remedial needs. If, however, as Warnock said, up to 20 per cent of *all* children were likely to have special educational needs at some time in their school lives, a revolution in remedial education was, of course, necessary. Most children with special educational needs will be found in the ordinary school, and it must therefore be the responsibility of the ordinary school to help these children; given the numbers thought to be involved this must be achieved via the regular school curriculum rather than by withdrawing children in ever-increasing numbers to specialists.

The Impact of Resource Cuts

As forced economies began to cut into the education service in the late 1970s, a number of LEAs began to consider ways of reducing their staffing bills. Remedial staff in many LEAs are part-time and/or on temporary contracts and therefore easier to shed than full-time permanent staff. Some LEAs cut their numbers of remedial staff, others looked for more cost-effective models of service delivery, some did both. One LEA was reported to be considering scrapping all, or much, of its remedial service (*TES*, 13 November 1981, 'Fewer books, classes and the end of farm studies'). Though this is not what has actually happened there did seem to be a mounting feeling of despair, at that time, about the impact of the cuts on the future of remedial provision. There was some evidence from teacher associations and HMI that the cuts *were* affecting remedial provision, but in a diffuse way.

In 1982 the NUT published the findings of a survey into the effects of expenditure cuts (NUT, 1982) based on information from its members. It presented a picture of larger classes, loss of peripatetic staff, reduction in supply staff, and head teachers required to do an increasing amount of teaching.

> Those who had suffered cuts said that the remedial service was one of the worst affected. Visits from remedial teachers have been eliminated completely in some schools and reduced considerably in others. Reduction has taken the form either of a reduction in the number of visits allowed by the remedial teacher or a reduction of the number of hours worked when she was in the school. Either way, the effect is that fewer children receive this form of help. In some cases the cutback has been extreme:

> 'Remedial help is non-existent now' (Infant school, Staffs)
> 'We have no remedial help at all' (JM&I school, Newham)
> '50 per cent cutback on remedial advisory service' (JM&I school, Oxfordshire).
> (NUT, 1982, p. 9)

> 'There is now a longer waiting period for supply teachers. This means that remedial teaching has to be abandoned until absent staff return. (Lower school, Northants). (*Ibid*, p. 14)

In early 1983 the NAS/UWT published a report of a survey which they had carried out among their members in the autumn of the previous year. The picture was one of reduced capitation in real terms (58 per cent of the LEAs surveyed), curtailment of in-service opportunities (41 per cent) an increase in the number of mixed-age classes in primary schools (57 per cent) and cutbacks in support/ancillary/peripatetic services (58 per cent of LEAs surveyed) (NAS/UWT press release, 17 January 1983).

In 1983 HMI also published a document on the impact of the cuts (DES, 1983). This was reported widely (for example TES and *Education*, 22 July 1983) and the report's findings on remedial provision were:

> the pattern of vulnerable subjects and groups of pupils is much as was noted last year with mathematics, science and remedial teaching significantly represented in both primary and secondary schools . . .
> Many primary and secondary schools have found themselves obliged by a combination of resource reductions and falling rolls to concentrate on the middle range of pupils with a consequence that the educational needs of the most and least able are not adequately reflected in either curriculum or organization. (DES, 1983 para 19 p. 12)

Thus the picture in the early 1980s was one of both general *and* specific pressures on remedial teaching and provision.

One outcome of pressures on staffing has been a tendency to develop changing models of service delivery. The most common change has been to alter the focus of remedial teaching services from having the child as client to having the class teacher as client, so that the service becomes one of support rather than teaching. This of course has cost-effectiveness implications in that one specialist can reach more children via a number of class teachers than she or he can reach direct. This, and other changes in the delivery or organization of support, are a major theme of our study and will be explored in detail in chapters 4 and 5.

An interesting side effect of the cuts has been the growing use of parents to help with reading particularly at school, but also at home. The involvement of parents with reading at home had of course been given educational approval by research carried out in Haringey (Tizard, Schofield and Hewison, 1982), Rochdale (Jackson and Hannon, 1981) and Hackney (Prosser, 1981). One of the great advantages for schools and LEAs is that parental help is free, (a point which has not been lost on its advocates, see Topping, 1985) and is in line with current moves towards increased parental participation in schooling.

A recent survey of parental help with reading *at school* (Stierer, 1984) found that just over half of the primary schools surveyed (202 or 53 per cent) also used parents to help with reading *in* school. The dominant pattern was for parents to hear the better readers, but a number of schools said that parents were used to hear poor readers and that this practice had arisen, sometimes against the better judgment of headteachers, because of cuts in remedial help.

The Effectiveness of 'Remedial' Education

Measuring the effectiveness of educational programmes is notoriously difficult. A major problem with evaluating remedial provision is that many of the 'experiments' or studies have been badly designed. The selection of children for remedial help is often unsystematic, while the 'experimental' treatment given is often difficult to specify, in terms both of teaching methods and of the underlying rationale (Cashdan *et al*, 1971). Also any gains shown may be due, not to remedial teaching, but to practice effects arising from using the same tests at the beginning and end of the study (Carroll, 1972). The Bullock Report acknowledged this in reviewing evidence on the effectiveness, or lack of it, of remedial education:

In seeking to discover the reasons for these seemingly depressing results, those responsible for the studies have drawn attention to the difficulties of making a just evaluation of measures which vary so greatly in approach and resources. Remedial education can consist of an hour or two a week in a centre or clinic or a daily period in school. It can be closely related to the rest of the child's work in school or it can be entirely dissociated from it, even to the extent of using a different orthography. It can range from unskilled treatment, based on inadequate understanding of individual differences, to expert help from a teacher with specialized training and long experience (DES, 1975, para 18.11, p. 271).

More recently, an American report from the National Academy of Sciences (Heller *et al*, 1982) has made the same point, that there is a problem in evaluating special educational programmes in that programmes can only be evaluated with respect to a properly identified class of children: if an instructional programme is not successful in a particular case it might not be that it is a poor programme, but that it has been applied to an inappropriate child or group of children. In addition, the content of a programme, or the children's actual behaviour within the programme is based only on a before and after picture, ignoring which features of the programmes are responsible for the observed outcomes.

Some findings can however be drawn from a number of carefully designed studies on the remedial teaching of reading. Remedial teaching can have dramatic short term effects but negligible long term effects (Collins, 1961, Cashdan *et al*, 1971); spontaneous improvement can occur if no remedial teaching is offered (Lovell *et al*, 1962); the variance among individuals in reading progress is often large (Moseley, 1969); attempts to predict which backward children are likely to make good progress are rarely successful, neither IQ nor personality factors having much predictive value (Clift, 1970); and once the remedial teaching is terminated there is commonly a decline in the rate of learning (Moseley, 1975). What these studies have established is that immediate gains in tested reading achievement can occur in response to remedial teaching but the long-term results tend to be poor.

It looks as though fairly intensive and long-term remedial support is necessary to effect improvement. A carefully designed experiment in the USA (Gittelman and Feingold, 1983) found that an individual intensive phonic teaching programme three times a week over a four-month period produced significant changes in the reading ability of children with reading disorders, at least up to eight months after the end of the programme.

However, even though this four month period of fairly intensive remediation was enough to have some effect on the children, it was not enough to make them average or even near-average readers. The ILEA reading surveys have shown that remedial teaching at secondary level is only effective if it is for a minimum of two hours per week (Woods, 1978), and for West Indian children at junior level for one hour a day (Mabey, 1982). Few LEAs, however, are able to offer this much help at junior level either individually or in small groups.

Small group remedial teaching of reading has traditionally been by withdrawal, ie children are taken out of class for teaching. Currently, new approaches concentrate on helping the child via the class teacher, by increasing her or his skills. An early attempt at this was made by Rutter and colleagues in their classic Isle of Wight study (Rutter, Tizard and Whitmore, 1970). They gave in-service training to primary school teachers and found that at the end of a year children in their classes had reading scores two months ahead of matched children in control classes. Interestingly, this research finding is rarely mentioned nowadays. More recently, in the Barking Reading Project, it was found that over a period of eight months children gained an average of twenty-two months in reading age when their teachers used a battery of diagnostic reading tests and associated reading material after in-service training (Trickey and Daly, 1977). There is some evidence, therefore, that this new type of approach can be effective in producing reading performance gains.

Using the class teacher as the primary support to a child also raises the possibility of extending the help from just reading to the whole curriculum, as the Warnock Report suggested. Tansley and Pankhurst (1981), in a useful review of research on learning difficulties, recommended that the focus be widened to areas other than reading; that special help be school-based; that assessment procedures be continuous, classroom-based and related to educational tasks. These recommendations are in line with current moves in practice, but there is little information on the likely effect of such changes.

Early Changes in Remedial Education

So much for the 'why', we now consider what form the changes were to take. The National Association for Remedial Education (NARE) had been discussing changes needed in the role of remedial education as early as 1975. A conference in 1975 was called 'Remedial Education at the Crossroads' and the title reflected the general unease that was sweeping through the profession, immediately preceding the worst of the education spending cutbacks. A second conference in 1977 took as its theme 'Remedial

Education: Guidelines for the Future' and the proceedings formed a book with the same name (Gains and McNicholas, 1979). There is a summary of guidelines at the end of the book which marked a radical departure from what was then generally considered to be 'remedial education'.

The President of NARE followed this up with an article entitled 'Remedial education in the 1980s' (Gains, 1980). He visualized three major developments: early identification and treatment; remedial work across the curriculum; and institutional change. It was the concept of remedial education across the curriculum which potentially opened up the most dramatic change of role:

> This could see an end to withdrawal methods, except in the most extreme cases. Here a child's needs are met in terms of his total tuition. The remedial teacher would act as co-ordinator, catalyst and resource agency. (*Ibid*, p. 9)

Remedial specialists could not stand by and ignore the changes that were happening around them. The dilemma of their changing role had eventually to be faced and solved; as Clark (1979) pointed out:

> Unless remedial specialists are alert to the implications for them of new developments . . . they may awake to discover that integration . . . has imperceptibly changed the type of children for whom they are responsible. (Gains and McNicholas, 1979, p. 23)

Others were also questioning the role of remedial teaching. In an important article in the *Journal of Curriculum Studies*, Golby and Gulliver (1979) opened up the whole question of what was to be thought of as 'remedial' — the child or the curriculum? Golby and Gulliver's argument was that children with learning difficulties are regarded by class teachers as individual failures in an education system which is considered to be basically sound. One of the historical props to this is the notion of normality (represented by the abilities and attainments of the average child) and abnormality (represented by the statistically less common pupils whose achievements are markedly lower). As an illustration:

> participation in a subject, such as history, requires a certain level of literacy, a level determined by the subject itself and the media through which it is taught. *Neither content nor media are regarded as open to change.* Those pupils who cannot meet this criterion are deemed in need of special help, and the improvement of their condition is to be achieved by remedial techniques which are not part of the normal teacher's function. (*Ibid*, p. 139, our emphasis.)

They also made the point that where full time special classes for children of low intellectual ability exist, placement in such classes is usually seen as a once and for all measure (so much so that if children do make dramatic improvements they are seen as mis-diagnosed in the first place). This is compounded by the fact that the curricula of the special and normal class are so different that transfer becomes less and less likely as time goes by. 'Remedial' with its notion of 'putting things right, rectifying and correcting' is therefore an unsuitable term for such provision as indeed was pointed out by Warnock (above).

The nature of remedial education was evolving at the same time as ideas were changing about reading, the major focus of remedial work at primary level. Through the 1970s there were changing attitudes to the nature and acquisition of literacy, and these inevitably impinged upon the debate about remedial help.

Changing Models of Reading

In the 1960s reading experts and teachers saw reading as a series of skills arranged in a hierarchical structure (Spencer, 1980). Reading was a matter of recognizing words: word recognition was the process and perceptual skills the vehicle of learning to read. Reading was divided into skills and sub-skills and teaching involved devising learning activities for the mastery of these skills. 'Look and say' and 'phonic' methods were derived from a decision about what constituted the smallest unit to be read the word or the letter (Moyle, 1982).

However, in the late 1960s and early 1970s, psycholinguists such as Smith and Goodman questioned the validity of these earlier models. Such models assume that written language can be coded into speech through phonic rules; yet in English, sound to spelling correspondences are unreliable, and total dependence on phonic rules is impossible (Hale, 1980). The psycholinguists suggested that as all communications were concerned with meaning, then meaning must have a central place in any theory of reading. What this suggested was that a teaching approach be sought in which the child masters the skills of reading within realistic and meaningful learning tasks rather than as isolated skill activities (Moyle, *op cit*). Others called on the importance of social relationships in the process of learning to read (for example Hale, *op cit*; Meek *et al*, 1983).

There are other debates about learning to read. Much of the recent research on reading has fallen into two groups — research on the problems of children with specific reading difficulties, or dyslexia, and research on parental involvement in reading which, as we pointed out earlier, is a growing practice. These two approaches are fundamentally different from each other in terms of their model of reading, one seeing reading essentially as a cognitive activity, the other as a social activity.

There are a number of recent reviews of these schools of thought: Cornwall, Hedderly and Pumphrey (1983) review the status of the 'dyslexia' versus 'specific reading difficulties' controversy; Bryant and Bradley (1985) review the psychological explanations for children's reading problems; Topping and Wolfendale (1985) review parental involvement in children's reading. These reviews are comprehensive and this is not the place to rehearse their arguments. However, an interesting study by Young and Tyre (1983) has combined the two approaches. A small group of children who had been identified as 'dyslexic' were involved in a programme which was able to improve their reading, through building on their existing reading abilities and involving parents for 30 minutes a day in reading tasks with their children.

To summarize, by the end of 1981 when we started this study there was a feeling that change in remedial education was necessary, and a number of ideas about how this might happen. It is clear, however, that there is still no consensus on the actual method of teaching reading to children for whom this is not an easily mastered skill. As for widening the province of remedial education beyond reading, practice was moving only slowly in this direction.

Now we turn to the question of who these children with special needs are, and who are to be the recipients of these new developments and approaches.

Special Needs

The term 'special needs' was first introduced by the Warnock Committee in an attempt to move away from descriptions of children based on a notion of handicap, and a categorization of their needs based on a deficit model. The term special needs was supposed to be wider, more general and to have positive, rather than negative, overtones. Unfortunately, the definition of special needs given in the 1981 Act is singularly unhelpful in providing guidelines as to who might be viewed as having these special needs:

> ... a child has special educational needs if he (sic) has a learning difficulty which calls for special educational provision to be made for him ... and a child has a 'learning difficulty' if ... *he has a significantly greater difficulty in learning than the majority of children of his age*. (DES, 1981, our emphasis)

Such a loose definition is nothing new; Cyril Burt also had trouble with vague definitions as far back as 1921. In those days the statutory definition was 'incapable of receiving proper benefit from instruction in the ordinary public elementary schools' (Burt, 1921, p. 167). The problem is that it leaves plenty of scope for idiosyncratic and subjective identification of these children by teachers. Croll and Moses (1985) in a recent study found that primary teachers when asked to identify children with special needs were most likely to identify those with learning difficulties (four-fifths of the children) and the most commonly identified learning difficulty was a problem with reading: nine out of ten pupils with learning problems and seven out of ten of *all* pupils described as having special needs were described as poor readers. (Behaviour problems were the next largest category of special needs and these children often also had learning problems.) However, while most children described as poor readers were at least one year behind their chronological age in reading age other characteristics of pupils and classrooms were found to influence teacher assessments. At particular levels of reading difficulty, children who were identified as poor readers were more likely to be boys, children with behaviour problems and/or younger children in the class. In addition (and this is not surprising) children in classes where the overall level of performance was high were more likely to be identified as poor readers than children with the same level of difficulty who were in classes where the overall standard was lower.

This sort of problem over the identification of children with special needs is not restricted to British children and teachers. In an American study of children identified as learning disabled (LD) in Colorado (Shepard, Smith and Vojir, 1983) the researchers found extensive 'mis-identification' of children. For example, in a representative sample of students already identified as LD fewer than half had characteristics associated with the state definition of learning disabilities. The researchers pointed to a lack of understanding about definitions and diagnostic indicators, on behalf of teachers and other professionals, and the power of social forces, for example pressure from parents to secure remedial services, as contributing to the mis-identification.

It is not only in the area of special needs that teachers are liable to categorize children on the basis of factors which are not entirely educational. A recent British study of the banding and setting of ethnic minority students found that West Indian children entering comprehensive schools with similar reading scores to those of white and Asian pupils were more likely to be placed in the lower band, with teachers tending to stress the poor behaviour of these children (*TES* 25 October 1985, 'Banding based on opinion of blacks' behaviour').

The three studies cited above do, of course, lend support to the now well-known arguments of sociologists such as Barton and Tomlinson (1981), that special needs are partly socially determined and that a separate system of 'special' education serves to maintain the existing social order. Better, they say, to question what is offered in the ordinary school if it is inaccessible to certain groups of children: comprehensive education hardly deserves the name if numbers of children are persistently failing and therefore excluded from it. This view has led to various attempts to change or rethink the curriculum and teaching approach in schools.

In addition, it is hoped that the integration of pupils with special needs will encourage similar examination of the curriculum and classroom management, and that this will encourage the move away from the traditional, medical, approach where the fault is seen to lie in the child. Potts (1982) suggests that teachers are relieved when a child is labelled as dyslexic or hyperactive, since they are then no longer responsible for the child's failure, as it is seen to be some problem inherent in the child. Indeed, in the USA it has been suggested that educators invented the term 'learning disabled' to provide a medical-sounding excuse for their failure to educate all pupils (Schrag and Divoky, 1975, quoted by Shepard *et al*, 1983).

Educational psychologists such as Wedell (1981), however, define special needs in functional rather than sociological terms: special educational need refers to the gap between a child's level of behaviour or achievement and what is required of him. This kind of definition leads in turn to an instructional one, since it suggests that the gap can be reduced by provision of extra or different teaching.

An instructional approach means the professional asking whether or not a child would benefit from (available) support such as individual tuition. The answer to this question is usually yes; there are very few children who would not, after all, benefit from such extra help. The danger is, however, that this may then broaden the definition to include any child brought to the professional's attention and the definition is then circular: a child has special needs because she/he would benefit from special help.

How Many Children?

Even if we were to have an agreed definition in educational, instructional or functional terms, there is still the issue of how wide a percentage of the population might be included. Since the 1981 Act places an obligation on LEAs to provide adequate help for *all* children with special educational needs, there are service-delivery implications.

The Warnock Report (DES, 1978a) concluded that one child in every five at some time, and one child in every six at any one time will require some form of special help. These figures are quoted in DES Circular 8/81, the

Circular to LEAs which preceded the implemention of the Act. The proportions given in the Warnock Report, and in particular the 20 per cent figure, are quoted regularly by LEA personnel, on whom the 1981 Act has had a considerable impact. Some LEAs are indeed using the 20 per cent figure as a baseline of provision for which to aim.

It is worthwhile therefore to take a look at where these figures came from. The authors of the Warnock Report drew together five sources of information on the incidence of special needs: the Isle of Wight survey (Rutter *et al*, 1970) mentioned earlier in this chapter, the Inner London Borough (ILB) study (Rutter *et al*, 1975; Berger *et al*, 1975), a study of children with special needs in the infant school (Webb, 1967), discussions with ILEA teachers (Inner London Education Committee, 1974) and the National Child Development Study (NCDS) (Pringle *et al*, 1966; Davie *et al*, 1972; Fogelman, 1976).

All the reported prevalences of special needs in these studies were between 12 per cent and 20 per cent. The Isle of Wight study, which gave an overall prevalence of 16 per cent, is the best known of these five studies and has provided a key model for other which followed, so we will consider it in detail.

The Isle of Wight survey gives us an 'objective' estimate of the prevalence of special needs because it uses measures from tests and rating scales rather than teacher estimates of need, or percentages receiving special provision as in the NCDS study. The problem with the latter type of information is that the percentage of children in provision is determined by the amount of provision available and to some extent this will also affect teachers' estimates of need. They are, therefore, somewhat arbitrary in comparison with percentages derived from measures of ability and attainment. But, we must ask, are the latter as 'objective' as is often thought?

When test scores or other measurements are used to determine the number of children falling into a particular group or category, for example intellectual retardation, a decision has to be made as to where we set the score which determines allocation to that group. The issue with these 'cut-off' points is that there are no absolute rules to determine where they should be set; it is essentially an arbitrary decision[1]:

> There is no infallible guide where to draw the line, . . . However, following Burt (1921) an IQ of seventy has usually been found to be the most suitable place to draw the line. (Rutter *et al*, 1970, p. 2)

Burt postulated that:[2]

> mental deficiency must be treated as an *administrative* rather than as a psychological concept. (Burt, 1921, p. 166, our emphasis)

and

> For immediate practical purposes the only satisfactory definition of
> mental deficiency is a percentage definition based on the amount of
> existing accommodation. (*Ibid*, p. 167)

and, as the special schools of London could accommodate only 1.5 per cent
of the child population, this is where Burt advocated that the cut-off should
be set. In Burt's day this was equivalent to a mental ratio of 69.4, that is an IQ
of 70. Sutton (1981) has shown that the figure of IQ 70 was taken from Burt
and used as the cut-off or borderline figure in many influential reports and
documents on special education. Thus 'it began to assume a reified existence
in professional folklore'.

So eventually a cut-off of IQ 70 was used by Rutter *et al*, evoking the
authority of Burt, who chose it because at the start of the 1920s
London's special schools could cater for 1.5 per cent of the school
population.

Of course the one in five and one in six figures are national averages and
hence will vary from one part of the country to another depending on social,
environmental and other factors associated with measured performance.
This is what Rutter found in the Inner London Borough which had twice
the prevalence of the Isle of Wight. Thus for example, in more advantaged
areas 20 per cent will probably be an overestimate for that population.

The point we are making is that the setting of cut-offs has always
involved some arbitrary decisions. Rutter *et al* make this plain, as does Burt.
The problem seems to be that subsequent commentators then forget these
strictures and treat cut-offs as having a substantive reality. What is worrying
is not so much the use of classifications based on arbitrary conventions, but
the failure to recognize the arbitrariness, or indeed circularity, which is
involved. Although evidence in chapter 2 and chapter 6 suggests that,
overall, 20 per cent is a figure commonly arrived at by teachers, the point we
are making is that the one in five and 20 per cent figures are not immutable
and should not be seen as target figures.

Summary

At the same time as the Warnock Report advocated changes in remedial and
special education, financial cutbacks made part-time staff likely candidates
for reduction. Additionally, concern over the effectiveness of traditional
remedial teaching made remedial teachers (and LEAs) aware of the the need
to change their role. Although Warnock made some suggestions for
developments in services, there was no agreement on the best/most effective
way to teach children to read. Indeed, as some of the studies reported show,

the most effective method did not involve remedial teachers at all, but parents. The rather loose 1981 Act definition of special needs did not help in this, and indeed to some extent further worsened the situation by introducing high outline or target figures based on arbitrary cut-off points.

Thus the scene was ripe for change although there was little consensus or information about how to change.

We hope to chart a way through this confused picture to show what changes were being made and what followed in their wake, but first we look at screening in education.

Notes

1   This point is taken up again in chapter 2 with regard to screening.
2   For an expansion on this theme see GIPPS, C. GOLDSTEIN, H. and GROSS, H. (1985) 'Twenty per cent with special educational needs: Another legacy from Cyril Burt?', *Remedial Education*, 20. 2.

Screening and Identification

In 1980 our previous research found that the biggest single reason given by LEAs for the testing of whole age groups of children was 'screening'. Screening is the process whereby test scores or teacher ratings are used, either exclusively or in combination with other indicators, to identify *individual* children in need of closer scrutiny and ultimately special help. Screening therefore implies some sort of follow-up to the testing process, follow-up which we discovered was so often missing from other testing activities carried out in LEAs (Gipps *et al*, 1983).

Screening has been a vogue term in education for over ten years and it has attracted a certain amount of controversy. It is therefore worth looking at the history of screening in order to chart its progress and to assess its current status. In this chapter we shall take a look at screening and other methods of identification including curriculum-related assessment and linked teaching objectives. In the next chapter we shall describe, from our questionnaire survey, LEA policy with regard to screening and identification, over the country as a whole in 1983.

Methods of Identification

Screening

The term itself is borrowed directly from medicine; screening of populations is well accepted as a medical technique, for example, the testing of all new-born infants for PKU — phenylketonurea — a condition of the digestive system which, if untreated, can lead to mental retardation. If identified early, however, and a special diet given to the child, retardation can be avoided.

The same principle, that of early identification with an intervention which prevents a harmful later condition, was adopted both by health and social services in developing 'at risk' registers, and by education in screening and early identification procedures. However, because the identification and prediction of children at risk is a far less precise process than the identification of PKU or other physical conditions, screening in this area has not been as successful as it has in medicine. Large numbers of children were identified as at risk who did not later have problems and therefore had a label attached unfairly to them, and vice versa children who later had problems were not picked up by the early screening. Following this, educationists also began to question the use of screening to predict children's educational performance.

Below we shall examine why it was thought that screening could be used for prediction in education and argue that the evaluation procedure for screening tests resulted in the reinforcement of this idea.

At the start of the 1970s only a quarter of LEAs were carrying out some form of educational screening, according to a survey carried out by the DES (DES, 1972). The Bullock Committee, in their 1973 survey, found that although LEAs reported many systems for identifying children in need of remedial help, only a minority of LEAs carried out regular reading surveys (DES, 1975).

By the end of the decade, however, the proportion of LEAs testing for screening purposes had increased quite considerably. In a survey of LEAs the Evaluation of Testing in Schools Project found that in 1980 half the LEAs which tested reading used a checklist or test in the early stages of primary schooling to identify children in need of remedial help. Seventy-one LEAs had regular authority-wide testing programmes for reading and thirty-five of the LEAs reported using the reading tests for screening purposes (Gipps *et al*, 1983, *op cit*). A survey carried out in 1981 by the Division of Educational and Child Psychology of the British Psychological Society, looking at the role of the educational psychologist in the discovery and assessment of children requiring special education, found that eighty-one LEAs (78 per cent) used systematic screening procedures (Cornwall & Spicer, 1983). The most frequently used type of technique was a reading attainment test. In the survey which was carried out as part of the study described in this report, seventy-four LEAs (71 per cent) had at least one screening programme, and reading was again the most widely tested area.

Thus there has been a clear increase in the number of LEAs using reading tests for systematic screening purposes. One of the early factors in this increase was probably the Bullock Report itself which was in favour of screening procedures:

Early detection of educational failure is of the greatest importance and there should be a far more systematic procedure for the prevention and treatment of learning difficulties. (DES, 1975, para 195, p. 537)

Concern over the short-term success of traditional remedial treatment also contributed to the move towards early detection of learning difficulties with the emphasis on prevention of reading failure by the class teacher rather than its cure by the remedial teacher. As the Bullock Report put it: 'The screening procedure should be seen as only the first stage in a continuous process of diagnosis used by the teacher to design appropriate learning experiences' (page 538). By the end of the 1970s, the publication of the Warnock Report led to a widespread acceptance of the notion that a large number of children will have special needs at some point in their school careers. This hammered home the message that identification was a major issue and age-cohort screening programmes were, as we have shown, the method adopted by many LEAs to help identify the 'one in five' of children with special needs.

There has been little evaluation of most LEA screening programmes (with some notable exceptions see Wolfendale and Bryans, 1979; and Rennie, 1980). This is partly because there are some major problems with the evaluation of such programmes. These are:

(i)   Evaluation of the screening tests themselves is often hampered by a lack of published information on reliability and validity (Lindsay, 1979). The small number of published instruments which do have such information are rarely used by LEAs because they are too expensive and time consuming (for example, Evans *et al*, 1979; Curtis and Wignall, 1981) the one exception being the Infant Rating Scale (Lindsay, 1980) which is both well developed and not too expensive in terms of time or money. Many LEAs use their own rating scales or checklists and these are usually not analyzed for reliability etc. As far as checklists are concerned the content of these has sometimes appeared so 'obviously' relevant that, to many originators of these procedures, it has seemed superfluous to ask whether they work (Wedell and Lindsay, 1980). The argument goes, as in medicine, that it would be considered unethical to design randomized trials for a procedure which has 'face' value.

(ii) The other problems all cluster under one issue which is that of the predictive model of evaluation used. The way in which screening programmes (and tests) are usually evaluated is in relation to performance on a second, related test, one year or so later. For example, scores on a checklist at age 5 or 6 will be compared with scores on a reading test at 7 or 8, or alternatively reading scores at 7 compared with those at 8 or 9. However, the few thorough studies that have looked at the efficiency of early identification procedures at the infant level have found that, although overall efficiency may be good, a high percentage of children who 'passed' the screening procedure later 'failed' in reading (Satz and Fletcher, 1979; Lindsay, 1980, *op cit*; Rennie, 1980, *op cit*).

The practice of using screening test scores to predict later attainment test scores has been called into question by a number of educational psychologists for a variety of reasons (for a most comprehensive review see Lindsay and Wedell, 1982). These can be summarized thus:

(a)   This model assumes stability of children's cognitive development, a view which is by no means universally accepted. On the one hand, Tansley (1967) takes the view that there are critical functions which inhibit learning and maintains that it is therefore possible to identify children with special needs at a very early stage in their lives. On the other hand, a different view is taken by Wedell (1980) who suggests a model of compensatory interaction involving resources within the child and within the environment. This means that it is difficult to make predictions about outcome, since children can and do compensate for their deficiencies by using their resources, including of course the major resource of appropriate teaching.

(b)   It is of course very difficult to evaluate a screening procedure in this way if it results in an intervention which modifies the situation. This is what Keogh and Becker (1973) have called the 'paradox of prediction'; simply, once a child has been identified as 'at risk' it is likely that there will be some form of intervention (indeed this is the raison d'etre of screening) and this may influence the child's later test score, hence compromising the predictive validity of the instrument.

(c)   Prediction also assumes a relationship between the abilities measured in the screening test and in the later achievement or criterion test. For example at age 7 one can test reading and compare this with reading at age 9, but the further one goes down the age range the further removed are the component tasks one which children are screened from the final target task (which is nearly always reading). In other words, if the screening is at 5, the skill tested cannot be reading but must be other skills, some of which of course may be assumed to be pre-reading skills.

(d)   In the widely used 'hits and misses' evaluation the proportions in the different cells, or groups, (see figure 1 below) will depend to some extent on where the cut-off points are set, ie, the score at which the children are deemed to have passed or failed either the screening test or the later attainment test. As we have pointed out in chapter 1 the setting of cut off points is entirely arbitrary.[1] Also, this model ignores what happens to the child between screening test and attainment test. It is a 'black box' model in which we look only at inputs and outputs ignoring the processes which go on in between. Furthermore, if *any* test was given twice to the same children 'hits' and 'misses' would be expected because of the fluctuation in children's development and behaviour, *and* the unreliability of tests.

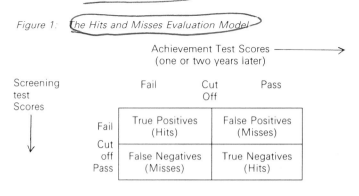

Figure 1: The Hits and Misses Evaluation Model

Achievement Test Scores ⟶
(one or two years later)

Screening test Scores

		Fail	Pass
	Fail	True Positives (Hits)	False Positives (Misses)
	Cut off Pass	False Negatives (Misses)	True Negatives (Hits)

(e)   Indeed, evidence from the National Child Development Study shows that only a small percentage of children in a national sample (5.1 per cent) were considered to have special needs at both seven and eleven (see table 1). Children who were in special schools or units *and* those children thought by their teachers to be in need of special help are grouped together in this table as 'SN'. The table shows a number of interesting things: first, that the percentage of children with special needs declined from 13.7 per cent at 7 (5.1 plus 8.6) to 10.6 per cent at 11 (5.1 plus 5.5); second, that the data implies considerable movement into and out of the special

Table 1:   *Percentage of Children with Special Needs at Ages 7 and 11, N = 12,736*

	SN at 11	*Not SN at 11*
SN at 7	5.1	8.6
Not SN at 11	5.5	80.8

Source: unpublished NCDS data

needs category, thus suggesting that a static 'hits and misses' model is unsuitable. The table also shows, of course, that approximately 20 per cent of children were classified as having special needs (5.1 plus 8.6 plus 5.5) at some point in their junior school career.

Despite the attempts of a number of educational psychologists to discredit the concept of predictive screening for individual children (see Moseley, 1975; Wolfendale and Bryans, 1979; Rennie, 1980; Leach, 1981; and Lindsay and Wedell, 1982) the notion of prediction has lingered on. This is, we believe, due largely to an artefact of the evaluation process itself.

In the absence of adequate research strategies, early studies to validate screening instruments looked at the later test performance of children earlier identified by the screening instruments as 'failing', that is, scoring below a pass/fail cut-off point on the screening test. Some children who failed the screening test were, however, later identified as good at reading; conversely others who 'passed' the screening test were later not good at reading. Both these groups would be described as 'misses', but the reasons for the pass/fail or fail/pass pattern *were never examined*. That some children should pass and then fail, or vice versa, is quite unsurprising and could be due to a number of things including: good or poor teaching; good or poor health; increasingly settled or unsettled home circumstances; spurts or lags in cognitive development; as well as technical inadequacy of the screening or later attainment tests. But it was always assumed that there was something wrong with the screening test because it was not predicting sufficiently accurately. Because this was the only method used to evaluate the instruments, screening became *ipso facto* linked with prediction; every time a screening test was validated the idea of prediction was reinforced.

Despite attempts over a number of years to point out that the predictive, hits and misses, approach was not a sound way of evaluating screening tests and checklists, studies are still being published which attempt to validate or discredit screening instruments via the hits and misses 'black box' prediction model (for example, Potton, 1983; Kingslake, 1983) and expecting a high predictive efficiency.

Kingslake (1983) in her examination of the predictive validity of a number of screening tests attempts to avoid 'the paradox of prediction' by saying that the pre-test post-test analysis only holds: '. . . in the absence of preventive intervention', between the screening and the later attainment test. This of course is quite unacceptable since it assumes that any action by the teacher is not of a preventative, or beneficial, nature. In fact this highlights the underlying illogicality of the predictive evaluation model when used to assess screening tests and programmes.[2]

The argument over prediction seems in any case to be particularly sterile since LEAs themselves do not view screening as a predictive exercise, but rather 'built in to the detection strategy of LEAs as part of the rationalization of the SPS's own referral system' (Cornwall and Spicer, 1983). For the rest of this report, then, screening, as practised by LEAs, does *not* imply prediction, but identification in the here and now.

In the wake of criticisms of screening and dissatisfaction with a system which identified but did not necessarily help, there has been a move towards assessment which describes children's strengths and weaknesses. As Lindsay (1984) puts it '. . . the child is seen as a changing person, for whom prediction is uncertain. Therefore, appraisal must be a continuous affair. . . . well proven screening instruments . . . must be incorporated into a continuous monitoring system'.

Early Identification

Increasingly, checklists or rating scales are being used particularly at infant school level to identify areas of development in which individual children may be making slow progress. This is often called early identification and the aim is to pre-empt teaching problems by enabling the class teacher to gear his or her teaching to each child's needs. These instruments usually involve teacher assessments of individual children's progress in various develop-mental areas including pre-reading skills. These are used both to identify children who may be in need of special help and also to make teachers aware of the child's strengths and weaknesses.

Identification, or early identification, then, is concerned with identify-ing children who have problems *at the time of assessment* so that intervention can take place. Several LEAs use early identification procedures to help teachers focus on relevant aspects of children's current learning (Cornwall, 1979) ie rather than for future prediction. For this reason, the argument goes, the information which the screening process produces should be linked to the curriculum, goals and processes of the school so that the teacher can take appropriate action. Since the class teacher is considered more and more to be the person most suited to deal with the child with special needs, and since many teachers have had little training or experience of how to deal with children with special needs, assessment in this situation does need to be curriculum related.

The Teaching Objectives Approach

As a result of this stress on curriculum related assessment, another recent development in LEAs has been the objectives-based teaching and assessment model, such as that used in the Special Needs Action Programme, (see Ainscow and Tweddle, 1979). This approach involves three strands: criterion-referenced assessment, precisely-stated objectives and task analysis. Ainscow and Muncey (1983) see the advantages of this approach as:

1 Assessment is classroom based and is the prime responsibility of the teacher.
2 Information gained from the assessment is specific and has direct implications for teaching.
3 Programmes of teaching objectives can facilitate continuous assessment and review.
4 They provide a basis for individualized instruction with pupils progressing at their own rate.
5 The philosophy behind the approach is essentially 'optimistic' in the sense that where pupils do not learn, there is assumed to be a flaw in instructional design, not necessarily in the child.

The growth of criterion-referenced assessment and teaching objectives in special needs stems partly from the objectives approach of much special education teaching, partly from the pedagogical view that clear objectives combined with feedback on progress are a necessary prerequisite for effective teaching (Cameron, 1982) and also from a genuine desire to develop assessment techniques which provide some feedback for the teacher. If 'all teachers are teachers of children with special needs' then the class teacher must be provided with assessment materials that are curriculum-based and therefore help her to design and implement teaching programmes matched to each child's special needs.

Of course the assessment process starts with the class teacher and any of the techniques described in the section above — screening, early identification, or criterion-referenced assessment and teaching objectives — could be used to help the class teacher with the identification and assessment of the child. Indeed all three processes can be viewed as operating within the same general framework viz:

screening and follow-up;
identification and intervention;
criterion-referenced assessment and the use of teaching objectives;

all operate on the same principle:

identify the child;
identify the problem;
do something about it.

In the next chapter we shall look first at LEA policy in identifying children with special needs, in particular screening programmes, and then at how teachers say they identify these children.

Notes

1 Although one standard deviation below the mean score is often used there is no reason for choosing one standard deviation as opposed to say two.

2 For a more detailed exposition of this argument see GIPPS, C. and GROSS, H. (1986) 'Screening and identification of children with special needs in the ordinary school', *Early Child Development and Care*, Vol. 24, pp. 43–62.

Chapter 3

How LEAs and Teachers Identify Children with Special Needs

LEA Policy in Identification

Turning now to what actually happens in LEAs we describe below the findings of our national survey. The questionnaire that we sent to all LEAs in July 1983 was returned by ninety LEAs — a response rate of 87 per cent — which is high for a national survey. Not only was the response rate good, but (as table 2 shows) all three types of LEA were equally well represented. As a result, we feel able to talk about the situation in the country as a whole.

The questionnaires were completed by a variety of people, but principal educational psychologists (PEPs) were most likely to be involved, completing the questionnaire alone in 26 per cent of LEAs, and with another person in a further 21 per cent of LEAs. Advisers/inspectors, alone or with another person, accounted for 20 per cent; a further 4 per cent were completed by the PEP and an adviser/inspector together.

The first question was whether LEAs had a 'screening/identification' programme, which we defined as 'tests and/or checklists given to all, or part, of an age group with the purpose of identifying children for remedial/special help'. The vast majority (82 per cent of the LEAs which replied, 71 per cent of all LEAs) did have such a programme.

Table 2: Screening Programmes by type of LEA

Type of LEA	Total number	Number of questionnaires returned	Number screening	Percentage screening (of total)
County	47	41	34	72
Metropolitan	36	29	24	67
London Boroughs (including ILEA)	21	20	16	76
ALL LEAs	104	90	74	71

The overall percentage of LEAs which screen is quite similar to the number of LEAs which tested in 1980 according to the Evaluation of Testing in Schools Project and the number of LEAs screening according to the survey carried out by the BPS (see chapter 2). Also, the percentage of LEAs screening is similar across the three types of LEA; metropolitan boroughs have the smallest figure but this may be affected by the fact that their response rate was lowest.

If an LEA has a screening programme it is likely to have more than one: 70 per cent screened at two or more ages, with one LEA screening at as many as six (see table 3).

Table 3: Number of LEAs having one or more screening programme

Number of screening programmes	Number of LEAs	Percentage of screening LEAs N = 74
1	22	30
2	20	27
3	18	24
4 + (max = 6)	14	19
Total	47	100

The most common ages for screening were top infants and first year juniors with 50 per cent and 49 per cent of screening LEAs testing at these ages respectively. The final year of junior school was also fairly popular (see table 4). Thirteen per cent of all LEAs with a screening programme include some testing at secondary level; however, no LEA screens only at secondary level.

Table 4: Ages at which screening takes place

	Number of LEAs screening in that year group	Percentage of screening LEAs N = 74
Infant 1	18	24
Infant 2	22	30
Infant 3	37	50
Junior 1	36	49
Junior 2	11	15
Junior 3	13	18
Junior 4	28	35
Secondary 1	4	5
Secondary 2	5	7
Secondary 5	1	1

As might be expected it is most commonly the whole of an age group that takes part in the screening programme; that was the case in over three-quarters of the 177 programmes. However, 11 per cent were voluntary (as far as the school is concerned, not the child) and 2 per cent tested only a sample of children, so they are not strictly speaking screening programmes at all.

In line with what is generally known about testing in schools, and about screening, reading tests are the most widely used instrument (see table 5). Checklists are the next most popular, with those developed by local authorities being much more common than the published variety. Maths tests are used too, but not on their own, ie they form part of a screening programme, usually in conjunction with reading tests.

Table 5: Types of test used in screening programmes

Type of test	Percentage of screening programmes made up of these tests N = 177
Reading test	46
Own checklist	18
Published checklist	4
Reading combined with another test, for example, maths	27
Maths test	0.5
Other, including behavioural assessment	6

Of the reading tests, Youngs Group Reading Test is the most widely used (see table 6). Choosing the screening instruments, whether tests or checklists, was likely to be done by the PEP (over half the LEAs mentioned this) with, in most cases, one or more of the advisers and/or a working party involved as well. In a further third of LEAs working parties, of unspecified composition, made the choice. In the vast majority of cases the tests are given *and* marked by the class teacher, often with the help of the headteacher. In only two LEAs was the test given by remedial/support staff.

Table 6: Reading tests used in LEA screening

Name of test	Number of LEAs using
Young's Group Reading Test	46
NFER Reading Tests, for example, A, B, C, D, E, EH1, EH2, Primary RT	48
Edinburgh	8
Carver	8
Spar	8
Burt	5
Daniels and Diack	5
London Reading Test	4
Neale	4
GAP	3
Schonell Graded Word Reading Test	2

It is interesting to note that many of the screening programmes are not particularly new. The most common recent year for introduction was 1978, although it was even more common for programmes to have been in existence before LEA reorganization in 1974 (see table 7). In fact, these screening programmes look remarkably like the testing programmes which LEAs told us about in the Evaluation of Testing in Schools project (see Gipps *et al*, 1983). The testing programmes we asked about then were for monitoring or accountability purposes as well as screening, providing information for transfer (at infant to junior, or junior to secondary level) and to help with resource allocation. One of the things we noticed then was the multiplicity of purposes assigned to those testing programmes, so it is perhaps not surprising that the screening programmes we were hearing about in 1983 are similar to the multi-purpose testing programmes we heard about in 1981.

Table 7: Year of introduction of screening programmes

Year introduced	Number of programmes	Percentage of screening programmes N = 177
1974 and before	47	27
1975	16	9
1976	11	6
1977	14	8
1978	23	13
1979	13	7
1980	17	10
1981	7	4
1982	7	4
1983	13	7
N/a	9	5
Total	177	100

Although many of the screening programmes are not new, almost two-thirds of the LEAs have changed their programmes in some way in the last five years. The changes have most often involved a change of test. In addition to this, over two-thirds are also planning to change their pro-gramme. These changes were in many cases still under review and were likely to be changes in the test used and age range covered, rather than anything more fundamental.

Checklists

Thirty-four of the LEAs used checklists as part of their screening procedure.

Apart from helping to identify children with special needs, or those who were having trouble with learning particular skills, almost all those LEAs using checklists reported that they were also for the purpose of sensitizing the teacher to children's development. Two-thirds mentioned record keeping and over half that it was an aid to curriculum development. All the LEAs said that they had supported the introduction of the checklist with in-service training, although naturally the extent varies among LEAs.

Other Methods of Identification

There were sixteen LEAs which did not have screening programmes and of these most (thirteen) did not have any plans to institute one either. One LEA had recently abandoned its screening programme because the reduction of their remedial and psychological service following the cuts had made it increasingly difficult to offer follow-up. All these LEAs relied on teacher or school referral either to the SPS or the Special Needs Support Service to identify children who might need additional help. This of course has always been the front line for identification of children, and 80 per cent of *screening* LEAs also mentioned this. In this situation the screening test results can be used as part of the referral process, or the referral may be taking place at a different age from the screening programme.

In addition, progress through a teaching objectives programme was mentioned by five screening LEAs and three non-screening LEAs. It is quite likely however that the figures underestimate the extent to which this method of identification is being taken up by individual schools, or in parts of an LEA, where an EP or an advisory teacher is particularly keen on this approach.

How Screening Test Results are Used

We asked the LEAs what the basis was for deciding whether children should receive extra support, although we realized that this would give only a very rough guide to what might happen in the schools. Not surprisingly the picture was a complex one. The basis most often mentioned (66 per cent) was a cut-off score, that is, all children below a certain score would automatically be investigated further; 46 per cent of LEAs mentioned that the test score and teacher's judgment combined were used to decide; but 55 per cent also mentioned that children would be put forward in consultation with the support services and it is not clear what the role of the test score would be in this situation. (In this question, as in many others, responses were multi-coded, ie respondents could give more than one answer so the percentage will add up to more than 100).

Interestingly, six LEAs said that whether children received remedial support depended on how much provision was available. In theory of course this must be the case for all LEAs, particularly those which have a policy of providing special help from outside the classroom, and we know that at least three LEAs work in terms of providing support for a fixed percentage of children, rather than those scoring below a cut-off score (though of course the two are linked in that a fixed percentage can be used to set the cut-off).

Educational psychologists have a central role in coordinating the identification of children and provision of extra help (in half the screening LEAs) together with advisers/inspectors for remedial or SEN (40 per cent of screening LEAs) and/or remedial support staff (in a third). Only three LEAs reported that no-one was responsible for co-ordinating the process.

Quite how the identification and provision processes follow on one from another was more difficult for the LEAs to describe. Answers given ranged from:

Metropolitan Borough
There is not currently available any remedial teaching. Any support is given by the educational psychologist or class teacher or both.

To:
County Council
(i)   Administration of the standardized reading test at 7–8 years.
(ii)   List of all children with RQ < 85, augmented by any children considered at risk by school staff.
(iii) Individual in-depth assessment by peripatetic remedial teachers with a written report containing recommendations. Referrals for further assessment/advice may be made to other agencies (for example, SPS, teacher of deaf, clinical medical officer).
(iv)   Appropriate remedial education within the limits of available resources arranged in consultation with the school and other agencies.

Via:
Metropolitan Borough
1   School/teacher same procedure.
2   School decides whether can cope within own resources.
3   School may contact remedial teaching area team.
4   Depending on needs/resource interaction help may be offered at individual, group or system level.

However, discussion between class teacher (and/or the headteacher) and a specialist (whether the EP or one of the special needs support team) is the main process by which it is decided whether children should have extra support or help. Some form of further assessment was also quite usual, about a third of LEAs mentioned this, as was using some kind of 'formula', for example, the use of a cut-off as already mentioned, or 'if any school has twenty children below the cut-off it is allocated a remedial teacher (from the central team)'. (As this last quote shows, sometimes the provision is for individual children and sometimes for schools). Only one LEA referred specifically to the Warnock stages of assessment here, though clearly the county LEA quoted above was using these stages, although they were not specifically identified as such.

Record Keeping and Evaluation

We asked LEAs about record keeping of screening programmes and any follow-up because we were interested to see what sort of evaluations were being carried out.

Only one LEA which screened kept no records of the results; in the majority records were kept both by the schools and the SPS/support service (60 per cent) while if records were only kept in one place they were more likely to be kept centrally (16 per cent) than in schools (8 per cent).

Although almost all screening LEAs kept records, only half made any sort of evaluation of their screening procedure. Of those with an evaluation, this was most likely to be made by the educational psychologists or remedial/support staff and to involve analysis of test scores. However, details given about this evaluation were not enough to be able to say very much about it, save that what is viewed as evaluation varies from an informal look at the children identified and their progress, to statistical analyses of screening and later test scores.

Fifteen out of the seventy-four screening LEAs actually described an evaluation which involved in some way analyzing scores on the screening test against a later follow-up test score. For example:

County Council
   Senior advisory remedial teacher did a follow-up of junior 1 'at risk' pupils on junior 4 test results . . . but to evaluate the teaching rather than the identification process.
County Council
   PEP and education officer have recently initiated follow-up of scores on subsequent tests.

Metropolitan Borough

> Screening test results compared with Carver (Reading Test) 12 months later.

Metropolitan Borough

> Summary sheet of all children's progress kept by head of (remedial) service. The PEP 'would dearly wish to' (do an evaluation of the screening/identification process).

and finally:

Metropolitan Borough

> There was an initial pilot project to develop/evaluate (the) identification scale. None further ie classroom observation scale is not intended to be used as a 'predictive' instrument, but an aid to structuring teachers' observations in the here-and-now.

Fewer than 20 per cent of screening LEAs were doing a pre-test post-test type of evaluation and of these only three mentioned the 'hits and misses' approach described in the previous chapter.

Indeed the last of the quotes above, together with these figures, support our earlier suggestion that most LEAs are not looking at screening in terms of future prediction, but for identification in the here and now.

Teachers' Methods of Identification

In our six case study LEAs we gave a short questionnaire to all the teachers in the case study schools (254 teachers responded in thirty schools, representing 87 per cent of the class teachers in those schools). One of the areas covered by the questionnaire was how the teachers identified children with remedial/special needs.

The major indicators across both screening and non-screening LEAs were personal judgment (mentioned by 86 per cent of the teachers) and a composite of child's progress/teachers' records (mentioned by 82 per cent of the teachers). Scores from tests or checklists came third with over half of the teachers using these (59 per cent, see table 8).

However, as the size of these percentages suggests, most teachers used more than one indicator. Only 11 per cent of the teachers used either personal judgment or progress/records alone, while only 4 per cent used test scores alone. Rather, the two major indicators were likely to be used in conjunction with tests/checklists (by 55 per cent of the teachers).

Over a third of the teachers (ninety-seven, 38 per cent) did *not* use test scores at all as an indicator, and the absence of an LEA screening programme appears to have had an effect here, as we might expect. In the three LEAs

Table 8:   How Teachers Identify Children with Special Needs

	Screening LEAs N=3 N Teachers = 139		Non-screening LEAs N=3 N Teachers=115		Total N=254	
	N	%	N	%	N	%
LEA test scores/checklists	77	55	–	–	–	–
Other test scores/checklists	62	45	57	50	119	47
(Any test scores/checklists	92	66	57	50	149	59)
Teacher's records/child's progress	108	78	100	87	208	82
Personal judgment	117	84	102	89	219	86
Other	6	4	15	13	21	8
N/a	2	1	6	5	8	3

where there was no screening programme (half the case study LEAs, but only 18 per cent of all LEAs in our survey) 45 per cent of the teachers did not use test scores, while in the three LEAs where there was screening a rather smaller proportion, 32 per cent, did not (see table 9).

Table 9:   Teachers' Use of Test Scores in Screening and Non-screening LEAs

	Teachers in Screening LEAs		Teachers in Non-screening LEAs		Total	
	N	%	N	%	N	%
Using test scores	92	66	57	50	149	59
Not using test scores	45	32	52	45	97	38
N/a	2	1	6	5	8	3
Total	139	100	115	100	254	100

In LEAs where there was a screening programme, the teachers who used test scores were quite likely to use both the LEA screening and other test scores (forty-seven out of the ninety-two teachers). If they did not use both, they were more likely to use the LEA test than another test (thirty and fifteen teachers respectively). However, we cannot say why the fifteen teachers who used test scores other than the LEA ones did so: it might have been because they did not like the LEA screening test *or* because it was not aimed at their age group of children. What we can say is that the presence of a screening programme in an LEA makes it more likely that teachers will use test scores. It does not mean, however, that teachers use only the screening test and do not use other tests. As we found in our earlier project, where standardized testing has a high profile as an LEA activity, teachers are more likely to do their own testing as well (Gipps *et al*, 1983).

The other point to make is that in screening LEAs teachers do not rely on the test scores as their only indicator of children with special needs. These findings tie in with those of Croll and Moses (1985) who interviewed 428 primary school teachers in ten LEAs across the country. They found that:

The procedure for selecting children to receive special help usually consisted of a consideration of both test results and the opinion of the class teacher.

In a few instances where no testing was done, the decision was based on teacher recommendation alone. In only one case were test results the sole basis for selection. ... both school test results and results of tests administered as part of an LEA screening procedure were considered. (*Ibid*, p. 85)

When our teachers were asked to say in an open-ended response how they identified children as needing *outside* help, they were much less likely to mention test scores (see table 10).

Table 10: How Teachers Identify Children as Needing Outside Help

Criterion used	Number of teachers	Percentage
Child's progress	118	46
Lack of resources/time	39	15
Discussion with colleagues	14	6
Test scores	12	5
Attainment compared to potential	9	4
Child is worried	14	2
'Experience'/vague answer	17	7
Combination of factors/other	20	8
Not the class teacher's decision	4	2
N/a	16	6
Total	254	100

The child's progress (or lack of it) was the main indicator, mentioned by almost half the teachers with lack of resources and/or time to help the child given by 15 per cent. Test scores were mentioned by only 5 per cent of the sample, but of course test scores may well have contributed to the teachers' views about the children's progress. Unfortunately we were not able to interview all the teachers to probe this issue.

Summary

Screening programmes are widespread with many LEAs testing at more than one age. The preponderance of reading tests in LEA screening programmes is not surprising given the central role of reading in the primary school, and the nature of most special help offered to children identified by this sort of programme.

We were, however, surprised to find so few LEAs using published checklists in their screening programmes. It may well be that this is because, as we have already pointed out, some of the published checklists are expensive and time consuming and may not be relevant to a particular LEA's needs. However, if increasing teacher awareness is part of the rationale for introducing checklists, then it is also likely that LEA staff will consider that developing a checklist is part of the in-service training programme.

The overall picture then is one of teachers using their own judgment, often assisted by test scores, to identify children with special needs, with teachers in screening LEAs more likely to use test scores. As chapter 6 will show, the teachers in our case study schools were by and large highly experienced. It is not surprising therefore that they should rely to a great extent on their own professional judgment to identify children with special needs and indeed, one might argue, it is appropriate that they should. That the screening test results were not the major referring factor would not surprise LEA staff either. Generally, the LEA view of screening programmes is that they are a safety net. Although there might be a seemingly cast-iron rule for identifying children, like a cut-off point, as we indicated earlier children thus identified would be discussed with the class teacher before any decision was made about extra help. However, one must question the commitment made by LEAs in terms of both time and money to screening programmes that appear to be of so little importance in the classroom.

Chapter 4

Provision for Children with Special Needs

Changing Models

In chapter 1 we examined some major reasons why remedial education came under consideration for change: concern about effectiveness, the impact of cuts in resources and the Warnock Report. In particular, the numbers of children that were likely to be identified as needing help indicated that the type of moves necessary were towards less staff-intensive models. It was also suspected that to be effective, the class teacher had to be centrally involved in the support process.

The Situation Before the 1981 Education Act

The Bullock Report outlined styles of provision:

> The arrangements for providing 'remedial' education vary greatly; from remedial classes or withdrawal groups within an individual school to peripatetic advisory services, area classes, or specialized help in remedial centres.
> (DES, 1975, para 18.10, p. 270)

The Report then went on to describe the patterns of organization and:

> approaches with which more schools might experiment, bearing in mind the essential condition that the teachers concerned should find it a congenial way of working. This is not to say that one system should simply be substituted for another. In some circumstances there may well be much in favour of the part-time or peripatetic teacher withdrawing individuals or small groups on occasions. What we are suggesting is a flexibility which permits a variety of practice.

At present the part-time teacher and the class teacher often work independently, and few schools have a member of staff with special responsibility for coordinating the work and advising. (*Ibid*, para 18.13, p. 272)

The Warnock Report described different models of special educational provision possible in ordinary schools rather more specifically:

(i)   Full-time education in an ordinary class with any necessary help and support.

(ii)   Education in an ordinary class with periods of withdrawal to a special class or unit or other supporting base.

(iii) Education in a special class or unit with periods of attendance at an ordinary class and full involvement in the general community life and extra-curricular activities of the ordinary school.

(iv)   Full-time education in a special class or unit with social contact with the main school. (DES, 1978a, para 7.12, p. 102–4)

Of these four models, (i) and (ii) are the most relevant to the group of children with whom we are mainly concerned. On the surface the models do not seem very different from what has been available for the last twenty years or so.

Between the time of the Bullock Report and the Warnock Report local authorities commonly had a remedial service which was run either alongside or as a part of the Schools Psychological Service (SPS). This service typically would include a number of peripatetic remedial teachers working to the principal educational psychologist or an adviser, often based in a remedial or learning or reading centre; some services had advisory teachers too. These were usually in addition to schools' own arrangements of part-time staffing or remedial classes.

Instead of the diverse groups of people with input into remedial provision, the Warnock Report suggested a rather more integrated approach and that every local authority:

should restructure and, if necessary, supplement its existing advisory staff and resources to provide effective advice and support to teachers concerned with children with special educational needs through a unified service. (*Ibid*, para 13.3, p. 253)

The support service which we propose would be made up substantially of existing advisers, advisory teachers and other specialist remedial teachers, reinforced by a number of practising teachers,

many of whom would spend part of their time in the classroom, or might be seconded to the service for a limited period. More staff will be needed ... but, for many local education authorities, the formation of an advisory and support service will entail in the first instance the re-organization and retraining of existing staff rather than the employment of large numbers of new staff.
(*Ibid*, para 13.4, p. 253)

The function of this special education advisory and support service would include: helping teachers to improve the quality of their teaching through the mediation of specialist advice and support; visiting schools to work with teachers in helping particular children; planning and organizing induction programmes for teachers taking up posts of responsibility for special needs; organizing short courses for teachers, ancillary workers etc; ensuring that schools are knowledgeable about assessment procedures. This range of responsibilities is then a considerable extension of the traditional role of a team of remedial teachers withdrawing children for individual help.

As far as the *legal* requirements of LEAs towards children with special needs in ordinary schools are concerned the 1981 Act and Circular 1/81, which accompanied it, did not have much to say. They are concerned much more with LEAs' duties and statutory procedures with regard to assessing and identifying the children for whom a statement of special educational needs is required. However, as a later Circular, 8/81, points out, the majority of children with special educational needs as defined in the Act will continue to be educated 'within the resources' of the ordinary school and it will not require the LEA to determine how their needs are best met (DES, 1981, para 9) ie they will not need a statement.[1]

Nevertheless, Circular 1/83 which considers the implications of the Act had more to say about the large group of children with special needs in ordinary schools:

the Act ... places a wider obligation on LEAs to secure that adequate provision is made for all children with special educational needs.
(para 2)

Since every school is likely to have some pupils with special educational needs, LEAs should provide guidance to all maintained schools in their area on the arrangements for identifying, assessing and meeting special educational needs.
(para 8)

Formal procedures are not required where ordinary schools provide

special educational provision from their own resources in the form
of additional tuition and remedial provision, or, in normal circumstances, where the child attends a reading centre . . .
(para 15)

However, the rest of the Circular is again taken up with the formal
statutory procedures for making statements of special educational need; and
the emphasis is on the assessment process rather than provision.

From the descriptions given above we can see that, before the 1981 Act,
provision for remedial needs, though varying widely, was generally based on
the withdrawal of small groups, or individual children, by peripatetic or
school-based remedial teachers; some LEAs also had reading or remedial
advisory teachers and reading or remedial centres. The Bullock and
Warnock reports advocated less withdrawal, an increase in advisory roles
and more flexibility. The 1981 Act itself simply encouraged a wider school-
based meeting of special needs, aided by an advisory support service, rather
than offering a prescription for change.

Changes in the Model

Whatever the official reports and circulars might say changes have been
occurring in LEAs' models of support for special needs in the ordinary school.
The main change is a move towards having the class teacher as the client of
the support service rather than the child.

The advantage of this model is that it enables the specialist support to be
more widely available. If a support teacher is working with individual
children the number of children that can be reached is smaller than if the
support teacher is working with the class teacher. By working with the class
teacher we mean offering support by providing materials, advice and in-
service training. By increasing the class teacher's skills, the class teacher
should be able to take more responsibility for children with special needs
than is the case in the withdrawal model. Of course, if the view is that as
many as one in five children may have special needs, then a model which
reaches more children (at less cost, preferably) is necessary.

Moving towards a model in which class teachers take on the main
responsibility for children with special needs is not unproblematic and of
course has implications for both teacher and child. The class teacher must be
persuaded that it is a good thing for her to take on this responsibility on top
of the other areas that she is being encouraged to take on more actively:
maths, computing, CDT and science (*TES*, 13 July 1984). Another
problem is that many primary school teachers like withdrawal, as we discuss

later (see chapter 6), particularly of children with behaviour problems associated with their learning difficulties (Croll and Moses, 1985) because it gives them a welcome respite. Class teachers will need practical help, advice and materials as well as training if they are to be expected to cope with this change and to make it work well.

The new model involves different skills on behalf of the support staff too. A peripatetic remedial teacher who has primarily taught individual children reading cannot necessarily be expected to have the right skills to advise class teachers on how to deal with a variety of individual problems. Their credibility in the eyes of class teachers may be at risk if this change is not clearly accompanied by some form of in-service training for the support staff. In short, this move, which looks more cost-effective (and indeed may be so in the long run) cannot be effected overnight nor without some expenditure on training and materials. As our case study of Norborough shows, there are many issues to be negotiated between support service and teachers if this kind of model is to be successful.

It is not just in this country that economic constraints are directing change in this area. In the USA a major report on mild mental retardation classification/placement stated:

> development of interventions in regular education as a first step is in line with current legal, legislative and professional opinion. Moreover, fiscal realities, in addition to perceptions of children's best interests, dictate greater use of interventions within regular education instead of referring all (or even most) problems to very expensive special education programmes. (Reschly, 1983)

It seemed then at the start of our study that there had been changes in the direction, and aims, of support services whether motivated by financial consideration, a desire for change, or both.

Current Provision in LEAs

To find out what provision was currently available and how the actual situation reflected changing models, the questionnaire which we sent to every LEA in England and Wales in July 1983 asked about their support services for children with learning difficulties. As table 2 showed, we received replies from ninety LEAs (87 per cent), with 87 per cent of counties, 81 per cent of metropolitan boroughs and 95 per cent of London boroughs replying. Of the LEAs which completed our questionnaire 97 per cent had a service (or more than one) dealing with children with learning difficulties in the ordinary school.

In view of our comments about changes in models of support, it is perhaps not surprising that two-thirds of these LEAs reported that their pattern of provision *had* in fact changed over the last five years. The changes were often poorly articulated on the questionnaire, but of those that gave adequate details, a move towards working with the class teacher as client was the most commonly reported change, in a quarter of LEAs which had made some change. This was followed by stopping withdrawal of individual children to units outside the ordinary school, in 13 per cent of the changing LEAs.

We asked what the services were called because of the changing terminology in special needs since the 1981 Act and there was a tremendous variety of names although Remedial Service was *still* the single most popular title (33 per cent). A complete list of names is in figure 2 and this gives thirty-five alternative titles, a surprisingly high number.

Figure 2: Names of support services
(in addition to Remedial Serivce)

Advisory Teacher Service
Area Support Service
Basic Skills Support Service
Basic Skills Support Team
County Reading Advisory Service
Education Support Service
Education Support Team
Language & Literacy Support Service
Language Support Service
Learning Support Service
Peripatetic Remedial Teacher Service
Progress Centre Advice Services
Reading Advisory Service
Reading & Language Service
Remedial Advisory Service
Remedial Reading and Language Service
Remedial Reading Centre
Remedial Support Service
Secondary Support Service
Service for Children with Learning Difficulties
Service for Learning Difficulties
Special Education Advisory Service
Special Education Service
Special Education Support Service
Special Education Advisory and Support Service
Special Educational Needs Service
Special Needs Advisory Service
Special Needs Facilities
Special Needs Support Service
Support Service
Support Teaching Service
Teaching and Support Service
Teaching Support Service
Tutorial Service
Tutorial Units

Although only one LEA used the name suggested by the Warnock Report (Special Education Advisory and Support Service), the words 'support' and 'advisory' do feature in most of the new names. The variety of names of the services suggested to us that there is an underlying confusion about the best way to restructure 'old-fashioned' remedial services. Such restructuring has had to take account of not only the Warnock Report and 1981 Act, but also the specific characteristics of individual LEAs and more often than not a lack of money for new posts or training.

These support services are most likely to be organized by the PEP and/or an adviser. It is less common for the PEP to head the service alone (13 per cent of LEAs), more often it is the PEP in conjunction with an adviser or the head of the service (35 per cent of LEAs). In few LEAs is it the responsibility of an adviser alone (12 per cent). It is interesting to note, however, that twelve LEAs had no adviser with responsibility for special needs at all; that is, they had no special education/remedial adviser or adviser for special needs. The number of staff in the support services — whether peripatetic remedial teachers (PRT), remedial advisory teachers (RAT) or SN support teachers — varied widely, from five or less in 18 per cent of the LEAs (including the three without a service) to over forty in another 18 per cent of LEAs (see table 11).

Table 11: Numbers of Peripatetic Remedial Teachers/Remedial Advisory Teachers/SN Support Staff in LEAs

				Number of Staff					
	0	1–5	6–10	11–20	21–30	31–40	41+	N/a	Total
Number of LEAs	5	11	14	20	17	6	16	1	90
Percentage of LEAs (N = 90)	6	12	15	22	18	7	18	1	100

Of those LEAs with over forty such staff one had 108 and one had seventy, so the variation in this group is also considerable. Looking at these figures by size of school population (primary and secondary) in order to make them more meaningful (see table 12) we find that the tendency, as we might expect, is for the smaller LEAs to have smaller numbers of staff and bigger LEAs, larger numbers. However, there are some important exceptions: four of the smallest LEAs have twenty-one or more support staff (one Welsh county and three London boroughs) while two of the biggest have ten or fewer (both of these are county authorities). Numbers do not seem to be simply related to the *type* of service in an LEA, so that some advisory services have few teachers and others operating on a similar model have many.

Table 12: Numbers of Peripatetic Remedial Teachers/Remedial Advisory Teachers/SN Support Staff by size of LEA

LEA size by primary and secondary population		NUMBER OF STAFF								
		0	1–5	6–10	11–20	21–30	31–40	41+	N/a	Total
Up to 36,000	N	1	6	7	3	3	0	1	–	21
	%	5	29	33	14	14	0	5	–	100
36,001–60,000	N	4	4	4	6	5	1	1	1	25
	%	15	15	15	23	20	4	4	4	100
60,001–100,000	N	0	0	2	8	6	3	5	–	24
	%	0	0	8	33	25	13	21	–	100
100,001+	N	0	1	1	3	3	2	9	–	19
	%	0	5	5	16	16	10	47	–	100

Although we also asked LEAs how many school-based remedial teachers there were (ie not centrally controlled peripatetic staff) four-fifths did not have this information.

In addition to changes in the pattern of provision, the majority of LEAs (79 per cent) had also had changes in their remedial/special needs staffing over the last five years. Where LEAs had gained staff these were most likely to be educational psychologists (57 per cent had gained educational psychologists). The reason for this was given as the increased need for assessment required by the 1981 Act. Apart from psychologists, there were gains in a range of staff from an adviser (in one LEA) to welfare assistants, but mostly support teachers of one kind or another. These were also gained because of the 1981 Act. Interestingly, few LEAs had lost staff because of cuts or falling rolls although a number had both lost and then gained staff (see table 13). The gains took place proportionately more in the London boroughs, while the losses occurred proportionately more in the metropolitan boroughs, though why this should be so is not clear.

Table 13: Staffing changes in the last five years, PRTs/RATs/SN support staff and EPs

	N LEAs	%	
Increase in staff	47	66	(10 mets, 24 CCs, 13 LBs)
Decrease in staff	9	13	(6 mets, 3 CCs, 0 LBs)
Increase + decrease	11	16	(6 mets, 4 CCs, 1LB)
Other	4	6	
Total	71	100	

Staff lost were most often support staff, for example, PRTs, RATs etc and not educational psychologists. LEAs seldom attributed staff losses to expenditure cuts *per se*: the situation is typically far more complex with falling rolls, cuts and reorganization of the service all playing a part. Although, as we showed in chapter 1, the loss of remedial staff in the wake of the cuts has been documented (NUT, 1982) it seems, from LEAs in which we have interviewed, that it is more common for schools to have had their general staffing cut, which has reduced the number of remedial or floating staff, than for the LEA to have lost remedial/special needs support staff.

As well as any increase in staffing which had already taken place, over a half of the LEAs were planning staff increases in the near future, because of the 1981 Act. Again this was most likely to be educational psychologists (35 per cent) but extra advisory/support teachers and remedial teachers were planned for a quarter and a fifth of LEAs respectively.

These responses, and the information about changes in the names of services, support the view that LEA support and advisory services were indeed undergoing considerable change in the early 1980s. However, while the pattern of provision was changing and moving away from withdrawal, particularly withdrawal to classes outside the school, the vast majority of LEAs reported that part-time withdrawal was still available in some of their schools. As table 14 shows it was available in 90 per cent of LEAs at primary, and 80 per cent at secondary level. *Full*-time remedial classes in ordinary primary schools were not unheard of either (41 per cent of LEAs reported having these).

Table 14: *Availability of provision*

| Type of Provision | Number of LEAs aware of this at: | | | |
| | Primary level | | Secondary Level | |
	N	%	N	%
Full-time remedial classes outside ordinary schools, for example, in progress centre	15	17	3	3
Full-time remedial classes in ordinary schools	37	41	55	61
Part-time withdrawal to groups *outside* ordinary schools	42	47	23	26
Part-time withdrawal to groups *within* the school	81	90	71	79
Special programmes for individual children in ordinary classrooms	69	77	54	60
Support to the teacher via advisory teachers, advisers etc.	78	87	63	70

At the same time too, large numbers of LEAs reported the presence of support to the class teacher via advisory teachers and individual teaching programmes in the classroom. However, these figures are very gross measures of whether a particular type of provision was available at all within an LEA and carry no information about how widespread that practice was within the LEA. But clearly, practice is diverse with varying facilities and different models operating side by side in some authorities.

Another development which we asked about was the extension of special needs provision to areas other than literacy, one of the major areas of development for remedial education in the 1980s. Half the LEAs reported that this had happened at both primary and secondary level, though how far these developments have gone in practice in those LEAs we cannot say. Two of our case study LEAs offered remedial teaching/materials in maths as well as literacy, though these were still in their early stages.

While LEAs, and schools, are changing the way that they help children with special needs, there was little information about the effectiveness of the provision made.

Of the ninety LEAs over half had no centrally determined procedure for assessing children's progress during the period in which they receive special help. Where there was such a procedure (thirty-eight LEAs, 42 per cent) tests were most likely to be used in the assessment (in 66 per cent of cases) and this was most likely to take place once a year (34 per cent) or once a term (16 per cent) and to be carried out by the visiting remedial/special needs support teacher (39 per cent). This then is a fairly traditional way of assessing progress. The more interesting feature is the fact that so many LEAs do *not* have a central system for keeping a check on children's progress. Of the LEAs with no central procedure, approximately one-third said that progress was monitored by the school, one-third that it was monitored by the visiting support teacher and the rest that this was 'informal' or varied. Of course where support is to the class teacher rather than to the child formal assessment of progress is not so simple, but few LEAs were actually operating this system fully at the time. All LEAs however said that records were kept of children receiving special help, whether these were kept by the school, the support service or by both.

Not surprisingly then, only thirty-five LEAs (40 per cent) made an evaluation of their remedial procedure. Again this was most likely to involve subsequent test scores (twelve LEAs) or to be an 'informal' procedure (six LEAs) although examinations and profiles were mentioned too (in two and three LEAs respectively). Of course, formal evaluation of the remedial process is not easy as we pointed out in chapter 1. Issues such as the nature of the children selected, how to assess process and evaluate outcomes are major research issues. However, at a simple level, asking whether the child has benefited from the support, or made any progress (over and above that which would have come from the ordinary classwork) must and should be asked. This presumably is asked in many cases even if it is done informally in the classroom rather than as a formalised, central, process.

As for how decisions are made about whether children should *cease* receiving remedial/special needs support, discussions with the support teacher or educational psychologist and the school, or the class teacher's view together with a consideration of the child's progress, or the judgment of the support teacher alone were the most likely procedures. Just under a third of the LEAs used either a cut-off score on a test to decide or a formula such as 'reading age equal to chronological age'.

Such cut-offs or formulae were thus more likely to be used in the process of deciding which children should receive remedial support (see chapter 3) than whether they should cease receiving support. More LEAs (eighteen) said that whether help stopped depended partly on what resources were available than those that said resources were a factor in deciding whether children should start receiving help (six LEAs).

We also asked LEAs what arrangements they had made or were going to make to ensure that 'adequate provision is made for *all* children with special educational needs'. Only three LEAs were still undecided (in the last six months of 1983) about any arrangements they planned to make. As for arrangements already made, a fifth of the LEAs had made changes in organization, while a quarter had provided in-service courses and/or information for teachers. A further group (27 per cent) were planning to provide in-service/information for staff and 14 per cent were planning a change in organization. This of course is in addition to the increases in staff described in table 13. The majority of LEAs had also done something about giving guidance to school governors — a half had actually given guidance, and a fifth were planning guidance — most commonly this entailed circulating them with a document detailing the points of the Act and how this would affect schools.

Circular 2/81 had suggested the possibility of using 'resources' freed by falling rolls for special needs provision. Almost half the LEAs had been able to do this. Of these forty-four LEAs far more reported using space (twenty-five, 57 per cent) than staff (seven, 16 per cent) although a small number (five, 11 per cent) had been able to use both. Given then that only twelve LEAs out of the ninety from which we had information were able to use staff freed by falling rolls for special needs, the suggestion from Circular 2/81, and indeed the Warnock Report, seem not to have been feasible as far as personnel is concerned, although this will have depended on local priorities.

There are those who viewed with disbelief the claims that changing special needs support could be achieved without extra cost, on the back of falling rolls. At the level of staff (freed by falling rolls) the cynics seem to have been correct. The situation regarding budgets and resource allocation at LEA level might be quite different but unfortunately this was not part of our remit and so we are unable to comment.

Summary and Concluding Remarks

The gross picture obtained from the responses to the questionnaire is one of variation and change. As was the case in 1975 (Bullock), there appears to be considerable variation in special needs resources and provision from LEA to LEA. Reorganisation of services, from remedial to support and advisory roles, along the lines indicated in the Warnock Report, is being widely undertaken. In many LEAs, however, old and new practices are going on side by side. As we have suggested, and the case studies will illustrate, such changes raise several issues of service delivery and may make it difficult for schools to understand what is happening or why. For example, it may be that as far as the LEA is concerned, restructuring a service, which involves removal of part-time staff in schools to join central teams, is part of a larger beneficial plan to support special needs and reach more children more efficiently. Schools however, may see this only as an effect of cuts in expenditure and have a negative response to the developments in general and the new central team in particular.

There have not been the cuts in central support staff that we might have anticipated on reading the educational press in, say, 1980. Most actual staff increases have, however, involved educational psychologists. The impact of increased numbers of educational psychologists on children with special needs in the ordinary school will in many LEAs be rather indirect and again class teachers may not realize or value this move by the LEA.

There have undoubtedly been changes in expenditure on special needs provision in LEAs. The most noticeable impact in schools however is the loss of part-timers, often used for remedial teaching. That this loss is just as likely, indeed more so, to be due to falling rolls is not understood by many teachers, and again the LEA is seen to be the villain of the piece. From the questionnaires and subsequent interviews it is clear that in some LEAs special needs money has been protected, because of the 1981 Act, and in some places extra money has been found. The fairest comment would be, we feel, that provision for the 'soft end' of special needs, ie the remedial child, has been protected in the face of economies because of the 1981 Act. Were it not for the changing climate towards special needs brought about by the Warnock Report remedial support services would, we suspect, have remained low status and been far more vulnerable.

As it is, in only a few LEAs is nothing happening regarding special needs in ordinary schools. Whatever the reason, models of provision and service delivery are changing and the moves are mostly in the same direction: towards the class teacher as client of the new advisory services.

The rest of this book describes and discusses some of the effects of these changes on teachers and children. In the next chapter we describe the models of provision in our case study LEAs.

Notes

1   Although it has generally been understood that the vast majority of children with special needs in ordinary schools should not be 'statemented', the recent judgment (TES, 13 December 1985) in the Hampshire dyslexia case implies that LEAs should provide statements of provision for all children with special educational needs. this would cause a substantial increase in demand for help from support services, of whatever kind.

Chapter 5

The Case Studies: Six LEAs

Six local education authorities were chosen as case study areas to represent different models of provision and identification, while covering a range of LEA type and part of the country (see Introduction for details). The aim was not to identify a particularly representative sample, and certainly not a random sample, but simply to illuminate a number of different policies. By describing, and commenting critically on, the policies which some LEAs have already taken up and the changes that have been involved, we hope to provide some sort of guidelines to LEAs which have yet to make policy/provision changes. (The detailed descriptions of the support services in these LEAs can be found in the companion volume by Gross and Gipps, *Supporting* Warnock's Eighteen Per Cent: Six Case Studies, to be published in 1987 by Falmer Press.

These descriptions are only of provision at primary level and although several of the LEAs had developments at secondary level we did not investigate them in detail.

Norborough

Norborough is a medium-sized metropolitan borough in the North West of England. The district is mostly industrial but includes a small rural area. However, the major characteristics of this borough are those of a typical inner city: declining industry, higher than average unemployment, a high proportion of working women, a mixed ethnic population and a large part of the housing stock Council-owned. Perhaps most importantly as far as education is concerned, it is eligible for extra money under the Inner Area Programme and Section 11 schemes.

In the special educational needs area, the borough has both special schools and special classes/language units. Ten years ago remedial provision in the borough consisted of one remedial teacher attached to the SPS. There are now two special needs support services — the Basic Skills Support Service (primary) and the Secondary Support Service which were set up in the school year 1983–84 and are directed by advisers.

The change from one remedial teacher to large support teams occurred gradually. Up to 1980 there was an enhancement on primary staffing for remedial support, with schools typically getting an extra 0.2 or 0.3 of a teacher. This was not so in all schools. As rolls fell, the numbers of these fractions of teachers declined and in 1980 it was decided that they should be put together to form full-time posts. These posts were allocated to schools with the most need by setting up units, ten altogether, which consisted essentially of one full-time remedial teacher in a particular school. Children from that school and nearby schools would attend the unit. Children were to spend half their time in the unit and half with their peer group in school. In order to reach more children, the units moved on to other schools after a year. However, there were still children who were not getting help and children in the LEA with a variety of needs which were not being met. So, although the units had been relatively successful and were liked, particularly by the schools that housed them, the LEA decided on a support service which would reach all schools and this was the new Basic Skills Support Team.

The staffing for the team consisted at first of the ten unit teachers, plus some peripatetic teachers who had worked with children with more specific learning difficulties, and five teachers funded by Inner Area money.

At the time of our visit the Basic Skills Support Team (BSST) consisted of a head of service, two area leaders and twenty-one teachers. When it started as a new service in the school year 1983/1984 it had two commitments: (i) to be in schools as quickly as possible (in order to compensate those heads who had lost the unit teachers); and (ii) to have a presence in every primary school in the borough.

The team operate from the Special Needs Resource Centre housed in a primary school near the town hall. The teachers are assigned to four to six schools each (every primary school is included) for varying lengths of time, ranging from half a day per week per school to two full days, depending on the school's need. Their role is to work with individual children and to give guidance and support to the class teachers.

Schools put forward the names of children whom they feel have remedial needs. There are 'screening' programmes in Norborough, at 7, 11 and 15 (ie the ages of transfer from infant to junior school, junior to secondary, and school leaving age) all involving reading. Results from the 15+ screening programme are used to pass on names to the adult literacy scheme. The infant and junior age programmes, which have been going for ten years or so, have been used in an undefined way to identify need, on the basis of children's measured reading age. But with the advent of the BSST LEA officers are uncertain about whether the screening programme is still necessary. It is thought that schools tend to refer children to the BSST on the basis of individual teacher judgement rather than screening results (this was confirmed by our teacher questionnaire survey).

Children put forward by the school are assessed by the BSST teachers on a variety of individual and group assessments; these assessments are all curriculum-related tasks *not* standardized tests. As a result of this children who are considered to need the services of the BSST are classed as 'recorded'. On the basis of the assessment a 'profile of independent skills' is produced for each child showing the skills which the child had already mastered; this is used as a baseline on which to build a teaching programme. Individual teaching programmes are produced for each recorded child consisting of lists of skills (a) which the child has mastered but needs to practice; and (b) which need to be acquired. Broadly speaking, the BSST teacher teaches these skills, usually in withdrawal sessions, and the class teacher then sees that the child practices those skills using material which the support teacher has identified or given to her. The aim is to move towards the BSST teacher working in the classroom.

Any child who is 'recorded' and helped in this way acquires a special record and the parents must be informed of what is happening. At any time when the class teacher or support teacher feels the child has made sufficient progress to no longer need the special help, a review is carried out. If a child's review is satisfactory and he/she is no longer 'recorded' the record has to be destroyed and again the parents informed.

The general technique of the service is to use highly structured teaching materials based on an objectives approach. The practice materials developed by the BSST are made available to schools: each primary school has a set of BSST support materials available for class teachers to look at and/or copy. At the same time as producing materials, the service aims to encourage school staff to use their own materials more effectively and cataloguing systems are available from the Centre to help in this. Any photocopying or purchase of BSST materials has to come out of the school's capitation allowance.

The BSST has spent more time and effort producing materials than they had expected to. The reason seems to be that in the beginning many class teachers were willing to cooperate and to do the practice work with the recorded children but felt that they did not have the right material. The support team produced materials working on the assumption that once class teachers got used to them they would work out which of their own materials would be suitable for teaching which objectives. Thus the materials are seen as a bridge to relate teaching objectives to a practical activity and teachers should eventually be able to classify their own teaching material which is already in the school. It does not seem to be the case yet, however, that schools have reached this stage: the expectation still is that the support service will provide ready-made materials.

As described in the next chapter about the teachers' views of the support services, the changes in Norborough have not occurred without difficulties. In the initial stages there was concern about the amount of time spent travelling from one school to another. This left both the schools and the team teachers frustrated at lack of time for liaison and may have contributed to problems of getting class teachers involved in the whole process from the start. This was not helped by some heads, who had lost part-time staffing or a unit, resenting the loss of control that a central team represented. In addition because of time spent making materials and doing assessments, the team was regarded as unreliable and some bad feelings arose.

All of these difficulties were to some extent inevitable in the changing of a service and in schools where there had previously been very little help reaction was generally positive. The support staff themselves were given some training initially and this was followed by regular weekly sessions at the Centre so that they could manage their new role as advice-givers.

The system in Norborough has been considerably extended from what was available five to ten years ago and it could be considered, by and large, to be fulfilling its initial intentions.

Southshire

Southshire is a large county area in the South East. It is an affluent county with lower than average unemployment, and 20 to 25 per cent of school age children going to the private sector.

In the special needs area it has a number of schools, units and centres both day and boarding for the deaf, partially hearing, physically handicapped, moderate and severe learning difficulties and maladjusted, as well as a number of remedial centres (RCs). There is also one teacher/adviser for remedial education and sixteen peripatetic remedial teachers (PRTs).

The policy in Southshire is to provide specialist off-site help for able children with specific learning difficulties whilst the schools themselves are expected to provide remedial help for slow learning/less able children.

The off-site remedial centres for children with specific learning difficulties were started in the mid-1960s. Whilst realizing that having separate centres for these children goes against the spirit of the Warnock Report the LEA has no plans to close or alter them since they are 'popular and successful' having built up considerable expertise; indeed any attempt to close them would be strongly resisted by the County's 'dyslexia lobby'. (In all the schools we visited the general feeling was that the RCs did indeed do a good job for the sort of child for whom they were set up, although the schools said that this was by no means the only group of children who needed help.)

The advent of the 1981 Act with its emphasis on the need to support *all* children with special needs, at the same time as cuts were reducing the amount of remedial work in schools, prompted the LEA to develop its remedial service. Thus in 1982 a peripatetic remedial service was set up to work mainly at secondary level, since the LEA was concerned that with the cuts and falling rolls a number of secondary schools had very limited remedial departments. The PRTs work with children and advise teachers and in many cases are used to continue help for children who have been attending the RCs as juniors.

The remedial centres take over 500 children from middle and sometimes first schools. Though they are geared for the average or above average IQ child with a reading age two years behind chronological age, this does vary somewhat from one centre to another. In the centres visited there had been changes in the type of child referred over the last few years and consequently staff are having to adjust to the idea of taking children whom they would not originally have taken.

In some of the centres there are a small number of children from private schools. The private sector has for some years used the LEA educational psychologists for testing of children, and using the remedial centres is seen as a logical extension of this. The LEA allows a small number of places to go to these children on the grounds that their parents are ratepayers and as such they are entitled to use the facilities which the LEA offers. (It might also be said that it is a matter of principle to show that LEA remedial centres are just as good as the private dyslexia clinics.) All referrals to remedial centres and PRTs are made exclusively by the EPs.

Each centre has a head and two or three teachers. In addition to the change in types of children seen, over the county as a whole the centres are apparently taking on the role of resource centres. Teachers come to consult with staff and use materials and it is likely that the centres' role will become increasingly outward looking. The teaching approach tends to involve structured, multisensory, and phonics approaches.

Peripatetic remedial teachers are based at the various remedial centres and in schools. Although senior officers of the LEA feel that the introduction of the PRT service had some problems — mainly an increasing tendency for heads to refer problems outside the school to the PRTs rather than to deal with them in school — there is a suggestion that the number of PRTs should be increased and this would provide increased remedial support to schools for children who are not referred to RCs. The new PRTs would be expected to work at secondary level.

There are two screening programmes — one in the last year of first school and one in the third year of middle school. At both ages the children take a reading test, maths test and IQ test. On the basis of the test scores EPs identify children with learning difficulties, and after discussion with the headteacher and class teacher, may refer them to a remedial centre. The LEA expects however the bulk of remedial support to be provided by the school. The IQ tests are used to identify high or average ability underachieving children and in this context IQ is seen as a significant measure. Indeed children were regularly described to us by teachers, heads and remedial staff in terms of their IQ score.

Parents play an important part in the remedial centres' work and teachers in schools are aware of this, although the teachers themselves are not usually involved. Parents are encouraged to take and collect their children where possible, and the three centres give the children homework. This often involves the parents in some way and there is a homework book in which parents write comments.

Liaison with schools is mixed; technically, all the centres visit the children's teachers somewhere in the first term of admission but it was the exception rather than the rule for us to talk to a class teacher who could remember a visit from the remedial centre teacher.

Overall the picture of the remedial centres in Southshire is one of well respected, highly specialized units which provide extensive help for the fairly small number of children who are lucky enough to get a place. Teachers themselves seemed to be split about whether it was appropriate to provide the most help for the brightest children, but they all felt that there should be more help available for the slow learning child. With the development of the remedial centres as resource centres, they will be extending their services to this group of children. In addition, the LEA's policy that the bulk of remedial support should be provided by the school will also be helped by the support and expertise of centre staff. The position in Southshire is one of gradual development of an existing system rather than radical change.

Suburb

Suburb is an outer London borough. The area is mixed, with a semi-industrial section and a large residential area. Much of the housing is Council-owned but there are few high rise blocks, it being mostly post-war estate housing with gardens.

As far as education is concerned, Suburb is known for the development of a scheme to improve children's reading skills developed over the last ten years. This project was developed under the auspices of the Schools Psychological Services (SPS) and is supported by a team of teachers attached to the SPS. A major feature of the scheme is the diagnostic assessment which forms the basis for individual tailoring of teaching material available from the SPS teachers. The scheme, which is voluntary, was set up by the SPS in response to the Bullock Report. With the shift in emphasis following the 1981 Act, the provision has continued to be regarded as appropriate and all primary schools in the borough, bar one, are now involved.

Despite the interest in children's reading problems demonstrated by the reading project, Suburb is one of the few LEAs that does not have an adviser for either special education or special needs or a special needs support service (although it does have a small number of special schools). This contrasts strongly with other areas we have visited where the policy towards provision for children with special needs has tended to result in either changes to the existing services or the development of a new support service.

Before the development of the reading project, teachers attached to the SPS visited schools on the basis of demand. Prompted by the Bullock Report and a growing interest in screening, discussions took place between the SPS and some primary heads. It was decided that they should try to develop their own materials for reading development. The intention was that the help should be available in the classroom through the provision of material and that any screening should have clear implications for teaching. The result of these discussions was the setting up of a screening programme using the Carver Reading Test for initial identification followed by a series of diagnostic assessments across the range of skills involved in reading.

Screening takes place in the first year of junior school. Children whose reading age on the Carver Reading Test is two years or more behind their chronological age are given the longer diagnostic assessment by their class teacher or the school's reading specialist. The assessment consists of tests of word retention, visual sequential memory, visual discrimination, sound blending, auditory sequential memory, auditory discrimination, concepts and vocabulary, and grapho–motor skills. The assessment and teachers' identification of which skills would be appropriate for the child to learn are then returned to the SPS. The specialist teachers check that the correct sets of materials have been requested by going through the individual assessments, and then send these out to the schools. They also discuss with the headteacher and/or relevant class teacher about how to use the materials and ways of working with the children.

Originally, the SPS sent out the appropriate sets of sheets from their master copies. However, to reduce costs, they have now sent out masters of the sheets for schools themselves to photocopy, thus also enabling some schools to be more discretionary and flexible in their assessment of children or in the use of sheets of work.

Help is given to children initially for a year at first year junior level. Assessment is built into the system of worksheets and some of the newer packs of materials which contain daily assessment tasks. In addition, whoever organizes the children's work at school, if this is not the specialist teacher, sets work for a week at a time and this must be checked when it has been completed. The specialist teachers do, however, keep a record and they may go in to the school once a month to check on the child's file and to see how they are getting on. Organization of help at school is left up to schools to arrange for themselves either in the classroom or in withdrawal sessions. At the end of a year of help children are retested on the Carver. If they have failed to make much progress, then they are considered for continuing help by the specialist teachers at the SPS.

The specialist teachers have both an advisory and teaching role, and they could be viewed as a special needs service in all but name. In the main, their teaching is not done in schools but is carried out at the Schools Psychological Service, where they are based. They teach in the mornings and make visits in the afternoons. They now only teach children from their own area schools who are brought up to the SPS by bus. The criterion for acceptance is that they are still well behind on the repeat screening at the end of first year juniors. Teaching is usually organized individually, so that each child will have his/her own work and the teachers will choose materials, or make them, to suit a child's particular needs. In addition, the teaching sessions allow opportunities for testing out materials that the teachers have been developing.

Theoretically there is a named person in each school who is the link with the SPS teacher, but this is not formalized and in most schools tends to be the head, unless the head has designated a member of staff for the role. Some schools do have a liaison teacher designated for contact with the SPS but there is no guarantee that this person will be available to see them when they visit the school.

Changes have been occurring in the borough. Some of these are in the special schools, which have been extending their contacts with ordinary schools and moving towards integration of some pupils. Others, which have occurred in remedial provision, mean that the SPS teachers now work in teams with an educational psychologist and are responsible for a set of schools rather than simply taking the next child on the list. New materials have been developed for use in schools and these have proved popular. The provision in Suburb is regarded largely by schools and the LEA as appropriate and adequate.

However, the emphasis is on reading and the materials available are concerned solely with reading. Special needs at the moment are still being thought of in a rather old-fashioned sense of remedial reading and provision in the LEA for children with special needs other than reading has been slow to develop. This is partly because the Reading Project already existed and could meet some of the needs. Nevertheless, there are several initiatives, particularly in special schools, to develop resources and there is considerable enthusiasm within the LEA for this type of development.

Ruralshire

Ruralshire is a large county area with a mix of rural, seaside and urban settings. The extent of its rural nature is emphasized by the fact that half the primary schools have under 120 children on roll and a number have fewer than thirty children. There are a university and a college of education to assist in initial and in-service teacher training but the geographical distances across the county make access to these and the teachers' centres a problem for many teachers.

The LEA is organized into four geographical and administrative areas and primary schools were visited in three of these. The PEP has responsibility for special education and works closely with the Remedial Adviser and the Adviser for Special Services. There are twenty-five special schools. There was a remedial service which is now called the Learning Difficulties Support Service.

The Education Committee at the time of our visits had a good record of protecting teachers' jobs (the PTR is the highest in that part of the country) but resourcing of schools was at a fairly low level. The cuts in educational expenditure had left their mark: a county-wide screening programme at junior 1 level was set up in 1978; however in 1981 this was dropped (in favour of triennial monitoring) on the grounds that there were insufficient resources to follow up the children thus identified. Partly because remedial and psychological services were overstretched, and partly because allocation of follow-up resources for schools diminished, the professional staff felt there was little point identifying the children if practical help was not forthcoming. The screening programme, staff felt, was raising false expectations so the decision was made to switch to emphasising informal identification, ie, teacher referrals to the remedial service and EPs.

The screening results were also used by the Remedial Adviser to allocate part-time staff, equivalent to approximately seventy FTE teachers, to schools in the greatest need. These teachers, mostly allocated in small amounts (ie 0.2, 0.5) are specifically to work with children with learning difficulties at primary level. As they are recruited by, and responsible to, headteachers there is no control over how these teachers are actually used in schools. Now the screening test results are not available, these posts are allocated in Area meetings involving the Remedial Adviser, the area advisers, the area EPs and area PRTs/RATs on the basis of local knowledge. Overall about one third of schools get some support of this kind so it is not an insignificant form of provision. The posts are relatively static but there is some movement, and head teachers are usually less than happy when this allocation is taken away from them.

In 1983 the remedial service consisted of ten peripatetic remedial teachers (PRTs) and ten Remedial Advisory teachers working mainly in primary schools, seeing approximately 400 children a week. (These two different types of post had resulted from the amalgamation of two different services in the 1974 LEA reorganization, one from two city areas and one from the old county.) As part of the LEA's response to the 1981 Act, during the school year 1984/1985 the remedial service was dissolved and the new Learning Difficulties Support Service set up. Most of the existing PRTs were phased out into part-time remedial posts in schools, although some of the staff were taken on in the new service.

The reorganized Learning Difficulties Support Service (LDSS) consists of, in each of the LEA areas, an Area Team Leader (scale 4), with a staff of scale 3s and 2s. The scale 4 appointments are new and three of the four people appointed are new to the county. As the new Area Team Leaders have come from different backgrounds and they have a certain amount of autonomy in a service which is new, there are different ideas about how they will operate. In one area, for example, the leader saw the team as testing children put forward by schools, monitoring their progress and visiting all schools in order to offer support and examples of good practice; some form of resource centre with an exhibition of material would be part of this function. In another area, where there was an existing team of PRTs, the plan was slightly different: to offer support to schools, but using the original PRTs (who will become remedial teachers in schools) in an advisory and coordinating role perhaps in in-service training, (although as scale 1 teachers they would need some preparation before taking on this sort of role). In this area the team leader and an EP had joined forces to operate 'support groups' for teachers from groups of schools. These involve 'contact teachers', ie, heads and/or interested teachers, going monthly to central meetings to learn about problem solving approaches and teaching objectives, to discuss common problems, plans and solutions. These were welcomed by heads and PRTs/RTs, particularly because of the regular support and liaison which they offered. At the moment the scale 2 teachers support class teachers who need a programme of work for individual children, but the aim is that class teachers will ultimately develop individual teaching programmes themselves.

Whether the LDSS in each area will visit schools on a contract basis, a referral basis or on a rotating in-service training basis was not yet clear, and each of the four areas may adopt different approaches.

The rural setting involving small schools and long distances provides its own problems for service delivery. The LEA is well aware of this and has various schemes to deal with it. This, however, can deflect attention from the small number of schools with inner-city type catchment areas on poor housing estates. Staff in these schools felt strongly that they were disadvantaged by the LEA in relation to the small rural schools; that they coped because the staff were dedicated but with minimal support from the LEA.

After some initial difficulties due to lack of resources (indicated by the ending of the screening programme) the LEA has responded to the demands of the 1981 Act and its local need by remodelling the support service, although there is considerable flexibility in the way that this will work. Staffing changes have taken place and at the time of our visit the PRTs were most concerned about their future. This illustrates clearly the difficulties faced by an LEA which wants to make fairly rapid changes to its support service: incumbent remedial staff have to be shed or retrained. If the latter course is taken it can be time consuming and may not work. If the former course is taken, because it is quicker or because the LEA feels a different type of person is needed, it will naturally cause resentment among the staff (and schools, if they feel they are losing trusted and valued help). Either way, a great deal of PR work is required of the LEA in such a situation.

Newtown

Newtown is a medium-sized city in the Midlands. The district is mixed: there is a largely residential area to the South and West of the city, however, the major characteristics of the area are similar to Norborough: declining industry, higher than average unemployment; a considerable ethnic population and a large proportion of Council-owned housing stock.

The city has always had a reputation for good provision for special education and there are a number of special schools as well as units for partially hearing, visually impaired and children with speech and language difficulties. As far as special needs are concerned, there is a team of four, the Special Needs Support Team (SNST), and recently there have also been teachers from special schools working in mainstream schools as part of an outreach project. The main thrust of provision for children with special needs in Newtown has not been through extending these services, however, but by encouraging mainstream schools to provide for children themselves within school. In order to do this, the LEA has developed a system of support involving an extensive in-service initiative, supported by the SNST. This initiative was planned to come into action with the 1981 Education Act and was started before the Act came into force in April 1983. Every primary school in the authority has now taken part and there is a well-defined system of special needs coordinators in all primary schools.

Five years ago, provision for children with special needs in mainstream schools was via a remedial teaching team which consisted of 10.6 scale 2 teachers. In addition to this team, all primary schools were allocated 0.4 of a full-time post above basic staffing (0.5 in priority area schools) to be used as the head wished and therefore may or may not have been used for remedial work in the school.

In 1980, as a precursor to the new initiative, there was a move to increase the advisory role of this team and four area leaders were promoted to scale 3 posts to spend more time working with class teachers and going into classrooms. Cuts in 1981 meant that the other six teachers had to be reabsorbed into schools, leaving only the team leaders (who now form the Special Needs Support Team). With such a small team, remedial teaching of reading on a withdrawal basis was impractical and the LEA was able to point out to schools how inefficient it was to use the team leaders to teach a few children outside the classroom. It was also pointed out how important it was for children's development in all curriculum areas that the class teacher was involved in a child's extra teaching. The essence of the in-service programme is that all teachers are teachers of children with special needs and the package aims to help class teachers fulfil this role.

In order to achieve these aims the programme has concentrated on four areas:

(i)   *information giving*: ensuring that headteachers and SN co-ordinators in the school are aware of all the resources and services that are available. To do this each staffroom has been equipped with a handbook detailing the location etc of support services.

(ii)   *in-service training*: courses are run for SN coordinators and then by them back at school to increase teachers' skills in developing and implementing programmes for children with special needs. A major aspect of the in-service training involves practical application of the theoretical ideas put forward on the course for dealing with problems arising in the classroom. Once the coordinator has attended the course, he/she is then responsible for making his/her colleagues back at school aware of their responsibilities towards children with special needs in their classrooms.

(iii)   the *materials* provided have been used and evaluated by teachers with experience of special education;

(iv)   schools receive *advice and help* from various, coordinated sources, including the four SNST teachers.

The SNST are based at the Teachers Centre which is in the middle of the LEA and easily accessible to all teachers. (This situation is in contrast to Ruralshire.) Each team member is responsible for quarter of the city's primary schools and they visit at least once every half term, and more often where necessary, to provide materials or advice. They keep copies of reading schemes, both commercial and home-grown, which they loan to schools. They also run in-service courses on different aspects of special needs, for example spelling. The team normally meets together once a week to discuss problems. Difficulties that have arisen for the team in schools rarely concern the change in role from teacher to advisory teacher, but are more practical, such as class teachers' need for more time to assess children and develop programmes of work.

There is no authority-wide testing programme in Newtown. The authority believes in context-based curriculum assessment, rendering any blanket testing policy obsolete. There is also some feeling in the LEA that screening by standardized testing is not necessarily an effective means of identification, particularly if there is no provision for outside help. Identification of children with special needs therefore occurs within school or classroom and methods vary from school to school. Schools may use the Basic Skills Checklist (BSC) to pinpoint exactly where a particular child's needs lie.

The Basic Skills Checklist is objectives based and all areas are presented as a series of graded steps; it covers most areas of the curriculum (language, reading, arithmetic, spelling and writing and social competence).

Identification and assessment of children who are on some form of special programme, following an objectives-based scheme, are thus semi-continuous; a child whose needs are identified through the checklist is then given an individual programme of work. This schedule of work may follow a 'small steps' approach, with each stage/objective clearly set out. Assessment is done as the child goes through these steps, since the child will not go on to the next step until he/she has successfully mastered the present one.

Assessment of children's progress can also be done using the Daily Measurement techniques which are introduced on one of the courses in the programme. This is similar to a precision teaching approach, where daily targets are tested, for example reading 100 words in one minute, until the target is reached. The Daily Measurement course was not as popular with teachers or coordinators as a method of assessment as was the use of the small steps programme alone.

In addition to the SNST and the programme decribed above, there are some more recent developments designed to help children with special needs in the ordinary school. These are the 'outreach project' and the 'visiting tutor scheme'. The outreach project is a method for creating closer links between special schools and mainstream schools to make use of the expertise already residing in special schools. The visiting tutor scheme, which has been set up since October 1984 is a response to demand from parents for some extra help for children who are not on individual programmes but whom they consider are in need of some help with reading particularly.

Change in Newtown from remedial teaching to an objectives-based teaching approach for class teachers, supported by advisory teachers, was planned carefully and took place in stages. The changes have occurred smoothly and this has been helped by the size of the LEA which means that communication is easy and information about new ideas could be got across. In addition all primary schools receive regular visits from the SNST. The LEA's support for the new initiatives is seen as evidence of the authority's commitment to special needs. Because the support service now visits every primary school regularly and is aware of how they are coping, and the LEA is seen to be positive about the new approach, special needs retains a high profile in school However, the work is still seen by some teachers as an addition to, and not part of, the child's normal curriculum.
not part of, the chiild's normal curriculum.

Midshire

Midshire is a large county in the Midlands, formed in 1974 from an amalgamation of the county with the city, the county town. There is a well established Literacy Support Service, a new and developing Special Needs Service and various pilot projects as well as a large number of special schools. In parts of the city there are high numbers of Asian children and there is a language service to support these children.

Midshire is perhaps one of the LEAs where major change has come about very rapidly, supported by considerable expenditure. These changes in special education provision stem from 1982 when the Education Committee became Labour-controlled. The Labour group felt that developments had to be made in special education and were aware that they might not be in power for long. Because of this, and because of the extent of change required, there was a certain note of urgency attached to the development of the special needs services.

The first move was to appoint an adviser for special needs who took up post in January 1983. The adviser came from outside the county and was appointed as a change agent with a brief to advise the Director of Education on what Midshire needed.

Pre-1981 the services to mainstream schools regarding special needs children consisted of the Schools Psychological Services (SPS), the Literacy Support Service (LSS) and seventeen FTEs allocated as hours to needy primary schools.

By 1985 there had been added to these existing services the new Special Needs Services, one arm of which is the Service for Children with Learning Difficulties. This consists of the Area Coordinators (ACOs) who coordinate local provision for children with learning difficulties, organize in-service training and supervise the Learning Difficulties Tutors. The ACOs were appointed from January 1984, which was a term later than anticipated, and unfortunately one term later than the LDTs whom they supervise. They are all local teachers: because of their role as coordinators it was thought to be important that they should understand the local area. They were appointed across a wide range of skills so that they could complement each other and balance their skills across the LEA as a whole. The LEA's idea is that the ACOs will go back into schools after a couple of years in this role, thereby increasing the special needs expertise in schools. The ACOs themselves have mixed opinions on this idea.

The LDTs, who were appointed (as were all the new staff) from within the County, were not selected as skilled remedial teachers but were given in-service training on the job. They work with 'named' individual children identified by the school and the ACO and EP. These tutors often only work with children for a short period of time and their role is seen by the LEA as essentially one of assessing the child in the school and classroom context. Some children may then be allocated further help, in terms of hours and this will be given by a teacher taken on by the school.

There is no centralized screening programme in Midshire, the aim being to encourage school based diagnostic assessment and to discourage schools from thinking that they can opt out of their responsibilities and hand over the children identified by centralized screening. The SNAP checklist and materials have been bought by the LEA, and the checklist modified to make it more appropriate for younger children. Each school has a link teacher who contacts the local Area Coordinator to discuss suitable ways of supporting children identified as needing help, preferably via the class teacher.

In-service training is seen by the new adviser as the central plank of the new support system, and the current special needs in-service budget is £60,000 per annum. In the school year 1984/85 over 2000 supply days were used for special needs in-service. Each term the Area Coordinators put on a range of in-service courses in their areas in response to schools' requests.

The original Remedial Reading Service which had been in existence since 1968 was renamed the Literacy Support Service in 1981 and gained six new staff, in response to the 1981 Act. This service had always been under the control of the SPS and these developments were quite separate from those in the Special Needs Services (SNS) under the new SN adviser. The LSS works with children of average or above average intelligence who have specific learning difficulties including dyslexia, offers in-service courses for teachers, and runs a resource centre containing assessment and reading materials. They operate on a part teaching, part advisory model. Referral can be made by anyone — parent, school, EP, doctor etc; most however, come from schools. Slow learning children are not the direct clients of this, or indeed any, service in Midshire, although it is hoped that the general in-service training, good teaching models, and advice offered will percolate generally to teachers of all children.

There is confusion in the minds of some schools as to which service children should be referred and some sort of clearing house is clearly necessary (the ACOs did this for a while, but the delays involved were unacceptable to the LSS). Since the LSS deals mostly with what we would call the '18 per cent' and the SNS deals mostly with the '2 per cent' in schools it seems surprising that in this post-Warnock era these two services should operate more or less independently.

The speed of changes in Midshire has led to a worrying by-product: that the staff employed in the new SNS were thought by schools to be of mixed quality. There were concerns voiced to us, at every level from schools to support services to professional and administrative LEA staff, about the expertise of some of the SNS staff.

There have also been some problems of role definition and overlap as the new service has several separate teams. Where there are no clear written guidelines on the roles of new staff there is bound to be overlap. Rapid growth is expensive in these terms. The LEA was of course in a double bind: if the money was not spent and the posts not established quickly they might well be lost in the next year's budget. There seemed to be a general feeling that by 1985/86 what was needed was a year of consolidation which would give the SNS time to establish credibility in the schools. It is taking some time for schools to realize that the special needs initiative in Midshire is one which encourages response from within schools. This is in any case not necessarily a message which teachers wish to receive.

To conclude, there is no doubt that change has come to Midshire, with tremendous speed and on a scale that would be the envy of many LEAs. However, this has not happened without cost to existing services and staff.

Overview

We have described six LEAs with differing forms of provision. There are however elements of similarity, for instance, Midshire's Literacy Support Service is very close, in terms of the children it reaches, to the remedial centres and peripatetic teachers in Southshire. A common move too, is for support teachers to advise rather than teach. Southshire in fact is the only one of the six whose peripatetic teachers still taught rather than advised.

As we indicated in the results of the questionnaire, the models of provision are indeed changing, whether the changes are dramatic, as in Midshire, Newtown and Norborough, or less so as in Ruralshire and Suburb, while in Southshire support is simply increasing. Two of the implications so far of the changes which we have described briefly were also that information about changes needs to be presented directly and clearly to all those concerned, whether support staff or schools; and that liaison time must be considered when scheduling visits of advisory/peripatetic remedial teachers, so that class teachers can discuss children and teaching materials with the new support staff.

The reasons behind the changes were rather hard to categorize, other than a combination of the 1981 Act and cuts. In theory changing to an advisory model will lead to an improvement in effectiveness but it is not yet clear how realistic this may be in practice. Certainly in LEAs such as Norborough and Newtown where every primary school now had some kind of support teacher visiting, levels of awareness of special needs had been raised. However, as the next chapter shows, the changes and increased support for children with special needs does not necessarily lead to satisfied teachers.

Chapter 6

The Teachers

Some of the people least likely to have been consulted about many of the new developments for special needs, but on whom these developments are dependent, are class teachers.

Chapter 4 has described how the implementation of the 1981 Education Act has led LEAs to review their provision for children with special needs, including those in ordinary schools. This resulted, in some places, in the setting up of new services and, in others, in the remodelling of existing services to take account of the demands made of them by the wide definition of special needs encompassed in the Act. In this chapter we look at class teachers' perceptions of these services and how their views about what they consider to be suitable ways of helping children coincide with what is available in their LEA.

One effect of the cuts has been that schools may have had their part-time staffing cut, so that they no longer have their remedial teacher who comes in every morning to take children for extra help in withdrawal groups. With the loss of part-time staff, who did withdrawal teaching, and the move towards LEA services offering advice rather than withdrawal, class teachers have become more involved in meeting children's needs in their own classrooms. This has resulted in increasing pressure on them to cope, while their views about these new developments, and the setting up of new services, have not generally been consulted. Decisions taken by LEA officers affect them directly and teachers' reactions to the LEA's support policy are likely to be rather different from those of the officers who made the decisions. It is a truism that unless class teachers cooperate, many of the developments in provision following the Act will not work. It does seem important, therefore, that teachers should at least feel informed about what is happening.

To investigate these differences in viewpoint we asked teachers in our case study LEAs, both directly and through a short questionnaire, what help they received for children with special needs in their classes and how they felt about this help. In addition we asked them what they considered to be the best way of helping these children.

The Teachers

The questionnaire asked teachers for details of their teaching experience, qualifications and numbers of children in their classes. Two hundred and fifty-four primary school teachers responded to the questionnaire. This was a response rate of 87 per cent. The schools involved were those selected for us by the LEA (see chapter 1 for details). Table 15 shows the details of the sample.

Table 15: Background Details of the Sample of Teachers (N = 254)

Distribution by age		
Age category	Number of teachers	Percentage
20–30 years	43	21
31–40 years	80	39
41–50 years	53	26
50+ years	30	14
Teaching experience in years		
Teaching experience	*Number of teachers*	*Percentage*
First year	15	6
Two to five years	47	19
Six to ten years	67	26
Eleven to twenty years	94	37
Twenty plus	30	12
N/a	1	0.4
Qualifications		
Qualification	*Number*	*Percentage*
Diploma	8	3
PGCE	17	7
BEd	33	13
Cert Ed	138	54
Other	10	4
N/a	48*	19

*Norborough teachers did not get this question.

The teachers were a highly experienced group: most were aged between 31 and 50 (65 per cent) and had been teaching for five years (75 per cent) or more, and half of them for more than ten years. The most common from of qualification was a Certificate of Education (Cert Ed, 54 per cent of the teachers), or a BEd (13 per cent).

Only 31 per cent of the teachers had had, or could remember having, any courses on teaching children with special needs in their initial training. Happily the situation with regard to in-service training was rather better: overall, 47 per cent of the teachers had been on courses in the last five years and this varied by LEA (rather than age, experience or other qualifications) (see table 16). However, 21 per cent of the teachers had had neither in-service training on special needs, nor any course on special needs or remedial teaching during their initial training.

Table 16: In-service training by LEA on Special Needs

LEA	Percentage of teachers in-service in last five years (N = 254)			
	Yes	No	No, but did before that	N/a
Norborough	38	47	15	–
Southshire	70	14	16	–
Suburb	29	61	10	–
Ruralshire	22	50	25	3
Newtown	65	32	–	3
Midshire	60	40	–	–
Total all LEAs	47	41	11	1

When LEAs responded to our LEA questionnaire in 1983 many of them (59 per cent) were still planning in-service courses (although a similar number had already given some courses) and it is possible that some teachers who would like to have attended in-service courses will have done so by now. However, as shown later, in-service training is not seen by many teachers to be among the most effective means of helping children with special needs.

The class sizes in the schools visited ranged from ten to thirty-six (table 17), the most common class size being twenty-nine. Classes were generally in year groups, but 27 per cent of the teachers in our sample taught mixed age classes. In some LEAs it was more than this: in Norborough and Ruralshire 45 per cent of the teachers taught mixed age classes.

Using a mixture of screening tests, other tests, personal judgment and

Table 17: Class sizes in schools visited

	Range	Most common class sizes
Norborough	25–36	29, 32, 34
Southshire	15–36	27, 33
Suburb	16–30	24, 25, 30
Ruralshire	10–36	26
Newtown	18–35	26, 28
Midshire	11–36	30, 29, 32

the children's records (see chapter 3), the class teachers identified varying proportions of the children in their classes as having special needs. While the range was from nought to twenty-eight, the most common number was five or six children. In a class of twenty-nine, this number represents about 20 per cent; a very familiar figure! As table 18 shows, almost a third of the teachers identified between 10 and 20 per cent of the children in their class as having special needs, with ten per cent of teachers considering the proportion to be as high as 30 to 40 per cent. In fact, the percentage of children went as high as 100 per cent (four teachers reported that all their children had special needs). This may reflect the vagueness of the definition of special needs but also, as argued in chapter 2, the proportion is bound to vary according to area. In some inner city area schools, there may be a case for considering all children as having special needs. The proportion identified by the teachers did not necessarily coincide with the number for whom they received extra help, in the form of extra tuition, materials or advice, (as the next section shows) and the effect of this on the teachers' feelings will be discussed later.

Table 18: Percentage of children with special needs in class

Percentage SN	Number of teachers	Percentage of teachers
0	7	3
1–5	26	10
6–10	22	9
11–15	40	16
16–20	42	16
21–25	30	12
26–30	15	6
31–40	26	10
41–50	17	7
50+	12	5
N/a	17	7
Total	254	100

The LEAs

The questions on the teacher questionnaire with which we are particularly concerned in this second were:

What do you think is the best way of helping children with remedial needs?
(rank in order of importance, ie 1–5 where 1 = best)
( )   withdrawal to regular sessions
( )   individual teaching programmes/materials

( ) assistance in the classroom with remedial children
( ) advice/in-service training for class teachers
( ) smaller classes so the class teacher can cope
( ) other (*please explain*)

Which of these statements best describes how you feel about the help you get?
(*please tick*)
( ) It is good, I feel on top of things
( ) It is adequate
( ) It is inadequate
( ) It is totally inadequate, I cannot begin to help all the remedial children

These questions may appear here to be rather stark; it should be remembered that they were embedded in the context of twenty-two other questions.

The options in the first question reflect the wide range of models of provision identified by our national LEA survey. As the type of provision varied from LEA to LEA, the questions were analysed by LEA and the teachers' feelings about the help, and how best to help children, are discussed by LEA.

Norborough

Norborough has a widespread new system of PRTs/RATs who at the time of our visit withdrew children in small groups for tuition and provided teaching material. The aim is that they should move to an advisory role, helping teachers to prepare special programmes and work alongside them in the classroom. This was not yet how most of the support teachers were working and, as answers to the questionnaire show, this is not what teachers in Norborough saw as the best way of helping children.

Forty-seven teachers responded to the questionnaire (this represented all the class teachers in the five primary schools we visited). Of the options suggested by the question, smaller classes were chosen as the best way of helping children with special needs by twenty-five of the forty-seven teachers. At the time of our visit, smaller classes were a major issue with teachers, since the PTR in the borough was poor (although it has since improved). Class sizes ranged from twenty-five to thirty-six (as table 17 showed) with the most common sizes being twenty-nine, thirty-two and thirty-four; these figures were the highest of our six LEAs. Forty-five per cent of the teachers taught mixed age classes and this, too, tends to lead to calls for smaller classes.

Withdrawal was also popular as a method of helping children, seventeen out of the forty-seven teachers ranked this first. As table 19 shows, advice/in-service training and assistance in the classroom were not considered as particularly helpful ways of dealing with children with special needs; advice/in-service training was not ranked first by any of the teachers. The new service was working by withdrawal and the popularity of this method means that the new developments, involving the support teachers working in the classroom alongside the class teacher and offering advice and materials for teachers' use, will have to be 'sold' to the teachers.

Table 19: The best way to help children with special needs: Norborough teachers' rank orderings (n = 47)*

Option	Rank order					
	1	2	3	4	5	N/a
Withdrawal to regular sessions	17	17	8	3	0	2
Individual teaching programmes/materials	3	9	15	18	1	1
Assistance in the classroom	3	8	14	13	5	4
Advice/in-service training for class teachers	0	2	6	6	30	3
Smaller classes so the class teacher can cope	25	7	4	2	6	3

*In this table and tables 21, 23, 25, 27, 29 and 32 the totals for each rank may not be the same as the total number of teachers, because some teachers gave the same rank to more than one option.

The response to the question on satisfaction (table 20 below) shows that, although these teachers like withdrawal and 70 per cent of them had children withdrawn at least once a week by the visiting support teacher, more than half of them were unhappy or dissatisfied with the help that they were receiving.

We know from our interviews that a particular area of concern was

Table 20: Teacher Satisfaction in Norborough (n = 47)

	Number of teachers	Percentage
Good — on top of things	1	2
Adequate	11	23
Inadequate	27	57
Totally inadequate	1	2
No response	7	15

liaison. The new support teachers have a heavy workload (approximately fifty to seventy children in two to five schools) and may not be able to spend much time talking to class teachers (although of course, some of them do find the time). This contrasts particularly with the previous arrangements in many schools which meant that there was a part-time teacher for remedial work who was in school regularly, probably every day, who got to know the children and the staff and was available in the staffroom during breaks.

The level of dissatisfaction for individual teachers did not relate to the proportion of children with special needs which they said they had in their class. There were as many teachers considering the help inadequate with less than five per cent of children in their class with special needs, as with more than thirty per cent.

Satisfaction, however, varied between schools; the teachers at one school seemed to be particularly happy with their lot. This school was working well with the new system and seemed to have got over some of the liaison problems. For instance, passing information about what the children were doing was done by writing in the back of the child's book and the class teachers were seeing more of the support teacher than in the early days of the service.

Norborough was providing help to every primary school via its support service and had put considerable resources into this service. Nevertheless although some teachers did think there was more help than there used to be, most thought that they needed more help than they got, ie that their help was inadequate, or totally inadequate. One might argue that all teachers will say they need more help than they get but this was not the case in all our LEAs. We believe that in Norborough, teacher dissatisfaction was partly because of poor liaison — always a difficulty with a peripatetic service — and partly because of prevailing concern over class size.

Southshire

Southshire has remedial centres, mostly at junior level, for children with specific learning difficulties and PRTs for withdrawal of the same type of child, mostly at secondary level. There are plans to extend this peripatetic service to reach more children. These services do not generally help slow learning children, who are the responsibility of the school, although the RATs do offer general 'remedial' advice to teachers.

Forty-three class teachers responded to the short questionnaire (this represented 83 per cent of all the teachers in the schools visited).

Table 21: The best way to help children with special needs — Southshire teachers' rank orderings (n = 43)

Option	Rank order					
	1	2	3	4	5	N/a
Withdrawal to regular sessions	20	4	8	4	3	4
Individual teaching programmes/materials	9	8	8	9	6	3
Assistance in the classroom	6	6	14	6	8	3
Advice/in-service training for class teachers	1	12	6	7	14	3
Smaller classes so the class teacher can cope	7	10	6	11	6	3

Table 21 shows that among these teachers withdrawal was definitely the most popular method of provision for children with remedial needs. Since Southshire is maintaining its remedial centres and expanding the PRT service, the LEA and the class teachers are in agreement over the type of service provided. Unlike Norborough, smaller classes were not seen as an issue, although class sizes in Southshire did not differ markedly from Norborough, ranging from fifteen to thirty-six, with the most common sizes being twenty-seven and thirty-three.

Despite the fact that class teachers thought withdrawal was a good way of helping children and many of them had children withdrawn for help (only seven teachers, 16 per cent, were not getting any help for children they considered needed it) they were no more satisfied, indeed slightly more dissatisfied, with the help on offer than Norborough class teachers (see table 22).

Table 22: Teacher satisfaction in Southshire

	Number of teachers	Percentage
Good — on top of things	0	0
Adequate	12	28
Inadequate	23	53
Totally inadequate	6	14
No response	2	5

Two-thirds of the teachers thought that the help was inadequate or totally inadequate. The satisfied teachers tended to have fewer children with special needs, but this was not always the case. Like Norborough, satisfaction seemed to be related to school; teachers at one school, which was middle class with few remedial children and a PRT two mornings a week, were more satisfied than others, which is perhaps not surprising.

Despite the general level of dissatisfaction our interviews showed that the teachers were fairly sympathetic towards the LEA because they thought it was having a hard time with resource cuts. Teachers were split about whether it was right to offer the most help to the children with higher IQs, as happens with the remedial centres, but all felt there should be more help for slow learners. Dissatisfaction was due, therefore, not to the type of provision, but more to the level of provision.

Suburb

Provision in Suburb is via diagnostic assessment and teaching materials, and advice to schools from the SPS and the SPS specialist teachers. After a year of classroom-based help from the class teacher, some children who have not made progress are given teaching help on a short-term basis by the SPS teachers at the SPS building. The help therefore combines some element of withdrawal with individual teaching programmes.

Forty-nine teachers from the five schools visited responded to the questionnaire, (this represented 80 per cent of the teachers). Like the majority of our teachers, those in Suburb had considerable experience. However, compared to Norborough and Southshire the staff were relatively young — 51 per cent were under thirty — and there were also five probationary teachers.

The rank ordering in Suburb was far less clear cut than in the other LEAs discussed so far (see table 23).

Table 23: *The best way to help children with special needs — Suburb teachers' rank orderings* (n = 49)

Option	Rank order					
	1	2	3	4	5	N/R
Withdrawal to regular sessions	15	11	7	4	9	3
Individual teaching programmes/materials	14	8	11	5	6	5
Assistance in the classroom	4	8	8	13	12	4
Advice/in-service training for class teachers	6	9	7	11	12	4
Smaller classes so the class teacher can cope	13	9	10	10	3	4

Withdrawal, which was common in schools as a way of using the materials (45 per cent of teachers had children withdrawn for help in school), and was part of the service offered by the SPS teacher, was ranked first by fifteen teachers. However, individual teaching programmes and smaller classes were also regarded as good ways of helping children with special needs. Class sizes in Suburb were amongst the smallest of the six LEAs: none was larger than thirty, so the issue of smaller classes was not as acute as it was in other LEAs with larger classes. Any preference for this probably therefore reflected the general desire of teachers to have smaller classes.

By and large the LEA is providing the type of service, or enabling the provision, that the teachers see as being useful for children with special needs: withdrawal, individual teaching programmes and smallish classes.

There was a fairly even split between those teachers who were satisfied with the provision and those who were not. This represents a higher percentage of satisfaction than in Norborough, Southshire, Ruralshire and Midshire but less than in Newtown (see table 24).

Table 24:   Teacher satisfaction in Suburb

	Number of teachers	Percentage
Good — on top of things	2	4
Adequate	21	43
Inadequate	20	41
Totally inadequate	5	10
No response	1	2

Satisfaction level was somewhat related to the proportion of children with special needs in the class, but the relationship is not a straightforward one: eight teachers who had 30 per cent or more of their children with special needs thought that the help was adequate.

Once again, within the LEA satisfaction was dependent on the school rather than the number of children with special needs. In Suburb two schools stand out. One school, where the staff were quite critical of the provision, had a part-time teacher who helped with the 'remedial' children by withdrawing them. This was not regarded as sufficient help for the number of children who needed it, according to the teachers. The other school, where staff were happier had, at the time of our visit, a spare teacher and several part-timers who helped with remedial work. This school was also involved in an outreach scheme from the local special school, for one of the junior children. Having more staff available to work with children with special needs obviously affects teacher morale. The use of such extra staffing also reflects the importance given to special needs within the organization of the school.

Withdrawal was a highly favoured option and heads are theoretically free to arrange withdrawal teaching from their own resources, but this is not always possible because some part-time teaching staff in schools have been cut in Suburb as elsewhere. This means that there was less withdrawal teaching available than there had been in the past and therefore a greater burden put on the class teacher. There was some complaint from class teachers that the SPS teachers did not realize how much extra time was needed to reorganize class teaching and to monitor children on individual teaching programmes, but overall these teachers were a satisfied group.

Ruralshire

Of our six LEAs Ruralshire is the one providing the least support to schools. The level of support varies slightly according to the part of the county, but the cuts have had a considerable impact. The support service is in a state of change: it includes a number of PRTs who are about to be lost while a new RAT system is introduced slowly and at no extra cost. However, there are part-time remedial teachers in many schools.

The number of teachers responding to the questionnaire was thirty-six which represented 90 per cent of the total in the five schools visited. They put withdrawal top of the list (see table 25) for helping children with special needs, but assistance in the classroom and smaller classes were also considered good ways.

Table 25:   The best way to help children with special needs: Ruralshire teachers' rank orderings (n = 36)

Option	Rank order					
	1	*2*	*3*	*4*	*5*	*N/a*
Withdrawal to regular sessions	11	5	4	3	8	5
Individual teaching programmes/materials	2	6	5	13	4	6
Assistance in the classroom	9	8	8	2	4	5
Advice/in-service training for class teachers	0	4	8	7	11	6
Smaller classes so the class teacher can cope	9	9	6	4	3	5

As this was the LEA where the largest number of teachers reported not getting any extra help (31 per cent) it was perhaps the case that any form of practical help, particularly people, would have been welcomed.

The LEA provision at the time of our visit did coincide with what the teachers most wanted; the problem, however, is that the plans for the new service will involve more individual programmes for children and advice to teachers. Both of these options were ranked very low in the scale by most teachers so that there is likely to be some opposition from schools to the new service.

Not surprisingly, given the availability of help, satisfaction amongst the teachers in Ruralshire was low (table 26). Ruralshire had the largest proportion of teachers (80 per cent) in any of the LEAs who considered the help received to be inadequate or totally so.

Table 26:   *Teacher satisfaction in Ruralshire*

	Number of teachers	Percentage
Good — on top of things	0	0
Adequate	5	14
Inadequate	22	61
Totally inadequate	7	19
No response	2	6

The teachers who were satisfied did not have a smaller proportion of children with special needs (one satisfied teacher considered that 30 per cent or more of her class had special needs). Satisfaction differed according to which school the teachers were in, no doubt partly because of the variation in support available according to the area of the county. At the extreme end of the scale, one school where all the teachers were satisfied, was a small rural school with only two members of staff. Although there were quite a number of children with special needs, there was a lot of support to the school. Staff were more dissatisfied in schools on large run-down housing estates and they felt that they were getting less support from the LEA than small rural schools.

The high rate of dissatisfaction is hardly surprising given the small amount of help that is currently available. Ruralshire was, until the 1985 local elections, a low spending Tory shire with a large number of small schools which are expensive to run. In 1983 it began to modify and develop its special needs services but they were starting from a very low baseline. The peripatetic remedial teachers were going to be disbanded at the time of our visit and the class teachers were disturbed about this. The small number of heads interviewed thought that the new services looked promising, but it is hard to know whether the teachers will feel any more satisfied with what they are offered than they do at the moment.

Newtown

Newtown has a special needs programme, via individual teaching programmes, which is supported by a team of advisory teachers covering all primary schools in the city. The city is also in the process of providing, in response to pressure from teachers and parents, an additional service of visiting tutors to help teachers in the classroom and to support children who still need help despite the teaching programme.

The number of teachers responding to the questionnaire was thirty-four (80 per cent of teachers in the schools visited). Unlike the other LEAs discussed so far, these teachers did not put withdrawal top of the list (see table 27). The best way of helping children with special needs was seen to be individual teaching programmes, so that like Southshire, the LEA policy is seen to be a good one by the class teachers. Assistance in the classroom was also popular, and the LEA has in fact recently provided some extra staff to help class teachers in the classroom. Smaller classes were not seen to be an issue although the range of class sizes in Newtown was as great as in Norborough (18–35, as table 17 showed).

Table 27: The best way to help children with special needs: Newtown teachers' rank orderings (N = 34)

Option	Rank order					
	1	*2*	*3*	*4*	*5*	*N/a*
Withdrawal to regular sessions	5	4	6	7	7	5
Individual teaching programmes/materials	13	5	6	4	2	4
Assistance in the classroom	10	8	7	2	4	3
Advice/in-service training for class teachers	4	4	6	7	9	4
Smaller classes so the class teacher can cope	8	5	8	7	3	3

The current system of helping children has only been in operation for a couple of years and the general feeling in Newtown is that teachers are willing to take on the responsibility for the children in their class with special needs, given the provision of help with individual teaching programmes. Newtown teachers were the most satisfied of all our six LEAs (table 28) — 65 per cent thought that the help was adequate or good.

Table 28: Teacher satisfaction in Newtown

	Number of teachers	*Percentage*
Good — on top of things	3	9
Adequate	19	56
Inadequate	10	30
Totally inadequate	1	3
No response	1	3

The preferred method of helping children was the one offered by the authority, and the high level of satisfaction contrasts with Southshire where the preferred method was also the one offered, but there was not enough of it. Over half of the teachers in Newtown received advice or materials from the support service and in addition half of them had children withdrawn for help by a school-based remedial teacher in their school. Only five teachers were getting no help at all. Even so, a third of teachers were not happy with the provision they got, one teacher considering that it was totally inadequate.

The dissatisfied teachers did not have a greater proportion of children with special needs in their classes, neither was there a distinct school effect in satisfaction level. At the school where teachers were least satisfied there were two special needs coordinators who helped with devising programmes, and it would seem that considerable effort and resources were being allocated to support children with special needs. It is therefore difficult to be sure why these particular teachers were not satisfied.

The dissatisfaction that did exist in the borough mostly seemed to revolve around the time needed to prepare the programmes and the feeling of being of under siege generally from other initiatives.

Interestingly in Newtown, where in-service training has had an enormous input, teachers were not particularly impressed with this as a way of helping children with special needs. It would seem that class teachers prefer some practical form of help, for example reducing their own workload by having extra staffing or by having some tangible form of help such as materials, or help with putting together the individual programmes. Or perhaps, as the key element of the in-service training was the teaching programmes, they did not see it as in-service *per se*.

Midshire

The last case study LEA, Midshire, is one of the few where a considerable amount of money has been found for special needs provision. This has led to the setting up of a range of new services for children with special needs of all kinds both at primary and secondary level. In addition, there is an existing specialist reading service (the LSS) for children with specific reading difficulties.

The number of teachers responding to the questionnaire was forty-five (87 per cent of all teachers in the schools visited). The new service for primary schools is one of PRTs who withdraw children for teaching help, as well as providing some advice and in-service training. As table 29 shows, withdrawal teaching is hardly the means chosen by teachers in Midshire as the best way of helping children with special needs. Instead they saw smaller classes as the best way. The range of class sizes in Midshire was eleven to thirty-six, with an average of thirty, so it was no better or worse than most of the other LEAs. As we pointed out at the beginning nearly all teachers would like smaller classes, but as our findings from Southshire and Newtown demonstrate, this is not necessarily a priority in relation to special needs provision. Assistance in the classroom was also thought to be a good way of helping children with special needs. At the time of our visit, the small

number of school-based part-time staff were being withdrawn from schools
to add to the staffing of the central support teams. This was not a popular
move. Help is also being offered to schools via advice and in-service training
from the new services, neither of which were favoured as options.

Table 29: *The best way to help children with special needs: Midshire teachers' rank*
orderings (n = 45)

Option	Rank order					
	1	*2*	*3*	*4*	*5*	*N/a*
Withdrawal to regular sessions	7	9	6	5	15	3
Individual teaching programmes/materials	5	9	13	10	2	6
Assistance in the classroom	12	10	4	11	4	4
Advice/in-service training for class teachers	4	4	8	9	13	7
Smaller classes so the class teacher can cope	20	9	7	3	4	2

The discrepancy between what is on offer and what is felt to be a good
way of helping children is reflected in the low level of satisfaction expressed
by the teachers in Midshire (table 30).

Table 30: *Teacher satisfaction in Midshire*

	Number of teachers	*Percentage*
Good — on top of things	1	2
Adequate	11	24
Inadequate	26	58
Totally inadequate	4	9
No response	3	7

Even with the considerable LEA expansion of, and input to, the special
needs services, two-thirds of the teachers considered the support that they
got to be inadequate. This is not as bad a situation as in Ruralshire (where
dissatisfaction was highest at 80 per cent) where there is limited help and
teachers are to some extent justified in feeling hard done by. It is however
high considering the commitment of the LEA in terms of resources.

Again dissatisfaction could not be related directly to the proportion of
children with special needs but there is some variation according to school.
At one, for example, where teachers seemed much happier there were a
number of school-initiated developments which were aimed at helping
children with special needs and the general atmosphere in the school was
positive.

Since the LEA policy in Midshire is not to provide masses of help
directly *to* schools, but to enable them to meet needs themselves with the
benefit of advice and teaching support, the LEA would probably see the

dissatisfaction as being a spur to schools' own developments. Indeed, in schools like the one mentioned above where there was some definite push or drive being made by the school itself, or where there were currently part-time staff used for special needs, teachers were more likely to be satisfied, regardless of class size.

Overview

It is clear that the teachers in the six LEAs had differing responses to the questions of satisfaction and the way to help children. When all of the responses are put together (see tables 31 and 32) the general impression is of teacher dissatisfaction with the systems operating in these LEAs.

Table 31: Teacher satisfaction — all teachers (n = 254)

	Number of teachers	*Percentage*
Good — on top of things	7	3
Adequate	79	31
Inadequate	128	50
Totally inadequate	24	9
No response	16	6

Well over half of all the teachers who responded to the questionnaire considered the help they received to be inadequate or totally inadequate, while a third considered it good or adequate. It is somewhat disappointing that given the developments in LEAs and the enormous efforts put into special needs only seven teachers (out of 254) considered the help they received to be good. This must be set against the general feeling of bitterness leading up to the industrial action in support of a pay claim which was a feature of schools during this period.

The response to the question on the best way to help children puts smaller classes at the top of the list, closely followed by withdrawal (see table 32). Advice/in-service training is at the bottom.

Table 32: The best way to help children with special needs — all teachers (n = 254)

Option	*Rank order*					
	1	*2*	*3*	*4*	*5*	*N/R*
Withdrawal to regular sessions	75	50	39	26	42	22
Individual teaching programmes/materials	55	44	57	49	25	24
Assistance in the classroom	44	48	55	47	37	23
Advice/in-service training for class teachers	15	35	41	47	89	27
Smaller classes so the class teacher can cope	82	49	41	37	25	20

The overall figures do suggest that teachers generally would like smaller classes, regardless of the kind of provision in their LEA, or the size of their classes. However, the detailed analysis showed that teachers in two of the LEAs (Newtown and Suburb) did not consider smaller classes as important as in the other four, and interestingly those teachers were also the most satisfied.

The continuing popularity of withdrawal raises several issues. The term 'withdrawal' of course covers a whole range of activities from a child going off-site for teaching sessions (for example Southshire), having a support teacher in schools withdraw children (for example Norborough and others) to having a parent in the classroom to hear children read in a corner of the room. Withdrawal has several advantages for the class teacher, whether he/she does the withdrawal or someone else: it allows the child the attention he/she needs without depriving the rest of the class; if children are difficult to manage it may provide a welcome respite for the teacher and the rest of the class. However, there is some concern that the popularity of withdrawal also indicates either the class teacher's feeling of lack of expertise or a reluctance to accept responsibility for that child's needs in class. Though many professionals might decry withdrawal of children, the information in this chapter suggests that there needs to be a dialogue with teachers if they are to accept this point of view. (We shall deal with this issue in more detail in chapter 9).

Looking at the average rank for each option, advice/in-service training for teachers is again ranked lowest (see table 33). Given that, as we have described, support services are moving to the advisory model this finding is not encouraging.

Table 33: The best way to help children with special needs: for all teachers (n = 254)

Option	Average rank (in order of preference)
Smaller classes so the class teacher can cope	2.46
Withdrawal to regular sessions	2.61
Individual teaching programmes/materials	2.76
Assistance in the classroom	2.94
Advice in-service training for class teachers	3.70

There may be several reasons for the rejection of in-service training or advice as a method of providing for children with special needs. One of these may be dissatisfaction with the advice and in-service that has been offered in the past. Class teachers whom we spoke to mentioned the lack of practical suggestions for help on courses which they had attended. As already discussed, problems of liaison and timing create difficulties for class teachers who receive help from peripatetic advisory staff and this may also have prejudiced their views about advice. Another reason may be the actual quality of the advice given. There was some feeling in one of the LEAs that support service teachers were not suitably qualified to give advice. Alternatively, the advice itself was not regarded as helpful by class teachers, who generally wanted practical help. This is no doubt why assistance in the classroom was more popular than advice, and why withdrawal, which has the added advantage of removing responsibility from the class teacher, remains so popular.

We have emphasized the teachers' feelings of dissatisfaction because we feel this is crucial. In some cases there were good reasons for it, for instance little help of any kind being forthcoming, as in Ruralshire, or help coming from the wrong sort of people as in Midshire. However some of the dissatisfaction resulted from more complex issues and to these we now turn.

Chapter 7

Implications of the Teachers' Feelings

As the discussion of the individual LEAs has shown in the previous two chapters, there are areas which have caused concern and difficulties for teachers in each LEA. Some of these have been because of changes in the system: in Norborough and Midshire, the withdrawal of schools' own remedial teachers has led class teachers to feel that they are not getting sufficient help from the LEA for those children they are worried about. Other difficulties have arisen because of the way the system works, for example visiting staff may not have time for liaison or to see all the staff in the school, as described for Suburb and Midshire. There are also rather more general issues such as feeling that the more a school does for itself the less support it receives, which is seen as inequitable, or that resources are being used wrongly — for instance on management rather than classroom help or materials. These are fairly standard reactions from teachers and cause little surprise. But there are other problems which have occurred in LEAs where new services have been developed and in this chapter we discuss some of these in detail.

New services that have been set up to work on an advisory rather than a teaching model may represent quite a change in role for the class teacher — as well as the support service (see chapter 4). It may also require an upheaval in the way that classes are taught and schools organized in order to make the help possible. These difficulties will affect the way the new system works, and the way it is perceived by the teachers.

First Impressions

Where a support service is changing its role in anything less than a painstakingly slow way, schools and teachers will need to be told and to understand what these changes are and mean. We believe that the experience in Norborough suggests that it is better in the long run to give the whole picture to teachers from the start rather than to let them in on the picture of change bit by bit.

The new support teachers in Norborough use a highly structured approach and the materials developed by the support service are left in schools for their use as well as for the support teacher to use. The children are given special (practice) work to do in class. In the best cases, this practice work is given and supervised in class by the child's own teacher. The committed class teachers will not only carry out this practice work but will also consult the materials which are left in the school and use those as and when he/she thinks they might be suitable.

However, as described in the previous chapter, there was a low level of satisfaction amongst the teachers in Norborough and although this varied from school to school, the support service had not been welcomed unreservedly. In part the dissatisfaction was because this was a new service, with resentment that schools had had to lose their own part-time remedial staff, and a feeling that this had led to less help and more work for schools. Since the teachers like withdrawal, there is no quibble with this aspect of the service. However, this is not the way that the service is intended to work. The aim is for the initiative to switch to the class teacher, with the help of the materials from the support service or the school's own material. The support service will then be acting in an advisory role, as their name suggests, rather than a teaching one. This is neither what class teachers appear to want nor have been led to expect.

The reason they do not expect it is because the support teachers spend all their time teaching and very little time advising. This is because teaching was seen, at the beginning, as a way in to schools, from which vantage point support teachers could then get their message across. However, although things are changing, there are certain problems. When the new service was set up there was pressure to use the allocated money sooner rather than later and it was cheaper and quicker to upgrade teachers already employed than to take on higher scale specialist teachers from the start. This meant that the staff were recruited largely as scale 1 teachers, who were not used to advising other teachers.

In addition, having got the staff, the service was immediately over-worked. Because a survey of needs produced many more children than they had expected, most of whom needed detailed and time consuming assess-ments, the staff could not get going as quickly as they would have liked. (The same happened in Midshire where the survey of needs produced many more children than the learning difficulties tutors could cope with.) Raising schools' hopes in this way was probably a mistake, since the service was then overwhelmed and the schools felt they had been either let down or misled, or both. Secondly, after less than a year in the schools, the support teachers were then withdrawn to carry out a maths assessment. The initial impression given to schools was therefore of a service that could not cope with the numbers of children the schools wanted, taught some of them for a short time and was then withdrawn. This first impression was therefore not a favourable one and certainly was not of a support service whose client was the class teacher. It was more of a 'hit and run' peripatetic teaching service with all the associated problems of unreliability. The problem for Norborough, then, is how to 'resell' the service to the schools as an advisory service. As support teachers are upgraded, it will of course be more reasonable for them to act in an advisory role.

The major difficulty stems from the initial presentation of the service. This is a recurring theme, particularly if change is occurring rapidly, for example in Midshire. It might have been better for Norborough to lay its cards on the table and to make it clear that the service was intended to reach class teachers rather than individual children, and to have presented the teaching as a back-up rather than the whole package. This would, of course, have meant taking on different support teachers, or starting off with a lot of in-service training. Certainly far more detailed forward planning would have been needed. However, the initial disappointment might then have been assuaged by the support teachers working in school with staff in an in-service, advisory capacity. This is what happened in Newtown.

Mismatch

Another specific issue is the mismatch between what is offered by the LEA and the way it is perceived by the teachers. Such mismatch has undoubtedly contributed to the (limited) feelings of dissatisfaction expressed by staff in Newtown.

Newtown contrasts well with Norborough because it took a very different line. The aim in Newtown was to make 'every teacher a teacher of children with special needs' and to do this they launched a major programme of in-service training, for representatives from each school. This representative may have been the Head but was in any case someone with status in the schools, for example the Deputy Head. This representative was then responsible for taking the information back to the staff in their school and selling the approach on to them. What they 'sell' is basically an approach to teaching. Like Norborough, this is a highly structured, teaching objectives approach, which takes the form of individual teaching programmes for children to master specific areas of weakness. These are backed up by practice tasks and tests to be done every day. The special needs coordinator (the representative in each school) is also responsible for helping class teachers to develop these programmes and for liaison with the advisory teachers. Organization is entirely up to the school unlike Norborough where because the support teachers come and teach on fixed days the structure is imposed by them.

When setting up the special needs programme, the LEA made it quite clear that the responsibility for children's needs rested with the school and the class teacher. There was therefore no misunderstandings of the role of the advisory teachers, although in schools where they had previously been doing remedial teaching, some conflicts of expectation between class teacher and advisory teacher had occurred, although these were rare.

Where misunderstanding does seem to have occurred is in the generalizability of the individual teaching programmes. The teachers were happy with the idea of individual teaching programmes as a way to help children with special needs. However, the impression was that they saw these programmes as something unique and separate that children should do in addition to their ordinary classwork rather than as an integrated part of their curriculum. by maintaining the individual programme as a special and extra thing for the child, the situation is analogous to that of the child who gets withdrawal help and who has practice work to get through before the next session. Indeed, this view was strengthened by some children *only* doing this work outside the classroom, in withdrawal sessions. The danger is that once the programmes are seen as separate it will become more difficult to extend the approach to other children, rather than easier.

Where programmes were working well class teachers had organized their class so that it was possible to sit down with an individual child to go through the programme without neglecting the rest of the class. However, one of the major criticisms by the teachers of the new system in Newtown was that they did not have time to fit the programmes in to the day. Solutions to the problem of fitting in this 'extra' work vary. One way of doing this, obviously, is for class teachers to let children get on with the work while the rest of the class are doing other more difficult work. Sometimes children may do their special work exclusively and then may miss out on things like 'choosing time', particularly if they are slow. An alternative to this is to do the special work at a quite different time, such as playtime or dinnertime. This prevents a children from joining friends and from playing and must be seen as the least satisfactory solution.

It seems that where the system was working in Newtown, class teachers had a flexible approach to classroom management, which suggests that advice about classroom management should have been incorporated into the in-service training package. As Newtown was the first LEA to adopt this approach wholesale they had no examples to build on and so criticisms are easily made with hindsight.

One explanation for the misunderstanding about generalizability may be the way that the information was delivered to the classroom. The LEA may have got the crucial message over to the school representatives who attended the course, but this may have got 'lost' when passed on to teachers back at school. For example, the message about the generalizability of the approach to other children and other parts of the curriculum, and that the programmes should be intrinsic to the child's curriculum rather than in addition to it. This 'watered down' version of the system received by most class teachers was therefore at odds in certain crucial ways with the message put out by the LEA. The 'watering down' of the message must be seen potentially as one of the weaknesses of the pyramid-selling approach.

This example of mismatch between what the LEA intended and the teachers' perception of it can again be traced back to the way that the message was put over to the teachers. As with the first impressions in Norborough, so with the watered down version of the in-service package in Newtown.

Other Reasons for Dissatisfaction

The answers to the questionnaires and our interviews with class teachers showed that even though LEA provision for children with special needs may coincide with what teachers thought was the best way of helping children, there may still be a degree of dissatisfaction with the help that is provided. This dissatisfaction is not with the *type* of service that is offered but the *amount* of it, such as the lack of resources to accompany a particular scheme. In Newtown, for example, although teachers were by far the most satisfied with what was provided, there were still complaints that there was not enough time to put together the individual programmes for children who needed them. Dissatisfaction may also of course stem from the perception that there is simply not enough help available of any type, and resourcing generally being considered inadequate, as in Ruralshire. The feelings of dissatisfaction in some schools extended to general issues such as help that was available going to schools which did not, according to the teachers, in some sense deserve it.

It was not possible to relate teachers' level of satisfaction directly to the type of help, amount of it, or even the age or qualifications of the teachers. Where the teachers worked, LEA or school, seemed to be most important. Of course, the number or percentage of children with special needs in a teacher's class must play a part; in classes where the reported proportion of children with special needs was as high, or higher than, 30 per cent, there certainly would not be enough time to get round to all the children on individual programmes, and teachers might naturally feel dissatisfied. Of course, this then suggests a need to reorganize the way the teachers manage their classes.

One thing in common among the three LEAs where least satisfaction was shown by class teachers — one of which provides a lot of support to class teachers and two of which do not — is that they have services undergoing change. It is not altogether surprising if this causes many of the staff to feel unsettled and dissatisfied, and some LEAs consider this to be a natural, even healthy, part of the process of change.

Pointers to Satisfaction

The two LEAs where most satisfaction was shown by class teachers were the metropolitan boroughs in which materials/teaching programmes are provided for class teachers to use themselves. It is, we would suggest, not so much that teachers do the work themselves that makes them feel happier about the provision but that these particular programmes/projects (as opposed to new services) were developed and introduced by the LEA in a positive, 'high profile' way. In both cases teachers have been involved in developing the materials, and the programmes have become well known outside the LEA. In Newtown, the development was LEA policy and the LEA is clearly committed to it. In Suburb, there is no LEA policy on special needs provision as yet but the project, which has been going for some time, had good publicity when it started and has continued to develop with support from the SPS. In both these LEAs the teachers feel committed to and, in a sense, proud of the programme because it is 'theirs', although there were also criticisms of course, as we have seen.

Neither Newtown nor Suburb are without problems. In Newtown there is some way to go before all teachers and schools will have come to terms with the organizational changes we feel are necessary to make best use of the teaching approach, but the attitude is enthusiastic. This contrasts with the feeling in Midshire which could best be described as disappointed and frustrated that the LEA has not 'delivered the goods'.

Furthermore, in Newtown, the change has not just been in the introduction of a programme, there has also been a wholescale change in the way the service is delivered and the onus for helping children has been put firmly on to the class teachers. By and large the class teachers have accepted this. We feel this is due to the positive and high profile approach of the LEA, its obvious commitment to the new approach, and its PR work. This again indicates to us that *how* the message is put across to schools is just as important as the content of the message.

Midshire, because of the huge financial commitment to special needs, also had a high profile approach but this has not lead to the same degree of satisfaction. Change has come quickly in Midshire, too, and we suspect that dissatisfaction has come about largely because of the LEA's failure to get their message across effectively. Newtown is small both physically and in terms of teacher numbers, so that for them giving out information is a much easier task than in large county LEAs. In Midshire information about LEA policy has only filtered in a very vague form to schools partly because of its size. Similarly in Ruralshire not only did many class teachers not know what changes were going on, neither did some of the PRTs But it is not just to do with LEA size, it is also something to do with responsiveness. In Newtown, where individual teachers have reached the end of their ability to cope, the advisory teachers have agreed to do some teaching, although it is not officially their role. By contrast the approach in Midshire appears to schools to be more along the lines of: this is what there is — take it or leave it, and it is not particularly surprising that teachers are not very happy.

As we suggested in chapter 6, class teachers are rarely consulted about what they would like. It is noticeable that where teachers have been involved in developments in an LEA, ie Newtown and Suburb, there is agreement between the LEA and teachers about the best way to help children with special needs and a higher degree of satisfaction with the help that is provided. It would seem to us that in setting up new services or changing old systems, it is important to involve schools and teachers at an early stage — if an LEA can carry the teachers with them a greater part of the battle for change has been won. This must involve in-service training at some point but as the questionnaire responses from some authorities have shown, this is not a highly regarded way of helping teachers with the children in their classes directly, since they would like more practical help. What is valuable about in-service training, however, is that it can be a way of communicating to teachers what the LEA policy is, and why they have chosen it. It is explaining their side of the new deal with teachers.

Given that the teachers' side in this new deal involves a considerable rethinking of their role with special needs children, it seems only reasonable for the LEA to explain widely, openly, and responsively, what both sides of the bargain entail. It seems to us that the worst approach is for an LEA to say: 'In the past you have referred remedial children out to experts (or at least another pair of hands). Now this is no longer acceptable practice (except for the very few) and you, the class teacher, must cope with all the children with special needs in your class,' and to follow this up with a bit of in-service training. Or worse still, not to say it at all but to change the system anyway.

Given the particular nature of the type of change we have described with its emphasis on the teachers' role, their feelings of dissatisfaction can hardly be in the best interests of the children.

In chapter 8 we consider the experience of children in receipt of these varying types of support, whether the teacher is the primary provider or whether help is provided directly by a support service.

The Children

Introduction

However an advisory or teaching support service is organized and however class teachers feel about it, the ultimate recipient of any provision is the child with special needs. In this chapter we consider how children fare under the different models of provision. In essence, our question was: 'What is it like for a child receiving special help?'.

To answer this question within the context of the LEAs we were visiting we carried out observations of children in their classrooms and wherever else they received special help, for instance units/centres or elsewhere in the school. Our intention was to locate the assessment and remedial procedure within the life of the classroom, whether this involved children being withdrawn from, and returning to, their classrooms, as in Southshire, or the teacher setting children off on individual programmes of work, as in Suburb. Our observation study aimed to illuminate and exemplify the ways that particular LEA policies were working at ground level. The numbers of schools and children involved are too few to permit generalization; instead we have sought to illustrate, through the use of 'pen portraits', examples of a range of practice.

Croll and Moses (1985) in a recent study of children with special needs in primary classes made detailed observations of seventy-one children with learning problems; they found that about a third of the children's time was spent in class activity and nearly two-thirds (64 per cent) working individually. Children with learning problems spent only a small amount of time (3 per cent) working in a group with the teacher and this was no different from the control children (ie, children in the same class not identified as having problems). This, of course, excluded time in withdrawal groups — which were the most common form of provision for children with special needs in the schools visited by Croll and Moses. Children with learning difficulties spent longer with the teacher *individually* (one to one interaction rather than as part of a group) than control children but not more than children with behaviour problems.

The majority of the children's time was spent in basic skills work, ie, mathematics, written work, and reading and other literacy work and this proportion of time was equivalent to that of the control children. They also report that children with learning problems spent a significantly greater proportion of their time distracted from their work than the control children and the time spent working individually was reduced. Moses (1982) also points to the increased proportion of time spent fidgeting by slow learners.

The results of the Croll and Moses's study indicate that the experience for special needs children is largely similar to that of other children in the class, although they spend more time with the class teacher as well as more time fidgeting, and being off task. The ORACLE study of primary classrooms by Galton *et al* (1980) found similar proportions of time spent in basic skills and contact with the teacher. We use these findings as a backdrop to our observations.

How We Did the Study

The one question posed earlier breaks down into some rather more specific questions, within different models of provision:

— how much time is the child with special needs spending on basic skills?
— how much time is spent on task, fidgeting?
— how is the class teaching arranged?
— how much time is spent in contact with the teacher both in class and in special groups?
— what is the level of curriculum overlap between class and special work?
— what happens when the child goes somewhere else for help (and when she or he returns)?

The details of the method of observation are given elsewhere[1], but briefly, a target child was observed in class and/or at a special session. The observations recorded curriculum activity as well as interaction with the teacher and level of involvement in work. Typically, an observation session lasted two to two-and-a-half-hours over two days, and would include following the child (discreetly) if she/he went out of the classroom for special help. Unless stated therefore, children were observed in class, and in receipt of special help, where this was different.

The children were chosen mostly from junior 1 or 2, after discussions with the class teacher, as those who most closely conformed to the idea of an average 'remedial' child and, where help was available, were children receiving this help. In addition to the target children (two per school), we also chose control children. These were the same sex as the target child[2] and chosen randomly from children seated near, but not at the same table as, the

Table 34: The children: basic information

LEA/child	Age at observation	Class/no	School/no	Provision/observation	Special characteristics
Norborough Stephen	9 years	J2/29	Primary 210	Withdrawal to support teacher once a week and practice work in class	
Southshire Ben	10 years	3M/34	Middle 380	Attended remedial centre two times a week (all pm) no carry over	
Donna	8 years	J1/20	Middle 300	Attended remedial centre two hours a week carry over by class teacher	
Suburb Kim	8 years	J2/25	Primary 350	Individual programme of work, done in withdrawal session with class teacher	
Ruralshire Sheena	8 years	J1/31	Primary 215	Half an hour three times a week to school's remedial teacher	At risk register
Newtown Wayne	8 years	J2/29	Primary 240	Individual programmes of work — organized and checked by class teacher; school has SN Coordinator	
Midshire Peter	8 years	J2/34	Primary 430	Twenty minutes four times a week with visiting remedial teacher and materials from outreach teacher for use in class	Quiet, but suspected hyperactive

target child. In total fifty-nine target children were observed together with fifty-nine control children, in the thirty schools visited in the case study LEAs.

Because we wished to explain rather than analyze we have not collapsed the data for all the children in an LEA and presented averages. We have instead chosen to describe in detail one child in each LEA. Thus the descriptions of the children, while typical of all those seen in the schools visited, are examples of how the different systems of provision could, and do, work. The children described as typical are children chosen by us, out of the target children in each LEA, who best exemplified the working of provision in that LEA as it had been described to us. The choice of children was therefore subjective, while the observations themselves were a relatively objective way of gathering information about the children and the system of provision within each LEA. Table 34 gives a brief summary of the children we describe and the type of help they receive; in Southshire we refer to two children. Descriptions of the provision available in each LEA has been given in earlier chapters (4 and 5).

The children described in the following pages cover a wide range of problems and need, but they are, we believe, typical of the sort of children primary teachers have to deal with every day in perfectly ordinary classrooms.

This chapter, including as it does narrative descriptions of the children's days, is a long one. Some readers may wish to turn straight to the overview on page 116.

The Children

Stephen: Norborough

In Norborough the target child, *Stephen*, was at a primary school where two support teachers from the BSST visited on different days. The school was newly built and open plan, with approximately 210 pupils.

Stephen was 9 years old and one of twenty-nine children in the junior 2 class. Since entering school in the infants, his progress had been rather slow and his records showed him to have been 'weak' in reading and maths and 'average' in written and oral ability. He was absent from the LEA screening in 1983 before junior transfer, but after a year in the juniors, when he was 8 years 8 months old, his reading age on the Schonell test was 6.2. He was assessed by the support teacher in his first junior year and this showed that he needed help in a range of areas: phonics, sight vocabulary and configuration.

He started seeing the support teacher that same year for three sessions a week and his teacher was pleased with the progress he made.

At the time of our visit and observations, Stephen was seeing the support teacher once a week, and doing follow-up work in class, using the Fuzz Buzz scheme of readers and workbooks. He was also reading other books in school, and was on Sound Sense Book Three.

When he was with the support teacher, he was one of a pair and they worked with some workcards that accompany the Fuzz Buzz scheme. The class teacher knew what work Stephen was doing in the withdrawal group, although she was concerned that time for liaison was short.

Stephen's day

In class Stephen sat with two other boys close to the teacher's desk. The teacher's way of working was to set up the work for most of the children in the class by going through it on the blackboard with the whole class and then setting different specific tasks for the different teaching groups. This then left her free to see the children who needed special help.

On the morning of the observation the class started with a spelling test and a tables test, which were a weekly occurrence. This was followed by English up to break and maths after break to dinnertime. Stephen did both of the tests and during English he worked with his Fuzz Buzz materials (a scheme used by the three children seeing the BSST), although he also did dictionary work together with the rest of the class. In maths Stephen also worked with the rest of the class, since they were all working through the same scheme at their own pace.

Stephen sat working quietly for almost the whole morning, at his place. He got up to see the teacher when she asked him to, and sat still with the whole class while she explained the maths work. When the tests were collected in, the teacher came over for a few minutes and sorted out with him what he was to do in his workbook. While working on this, he chatted and compared notes with his neighbour. The teacher called him out to check his work, she heard him read some of the words out, and then set the next piece of work. Children were all taking turns to read to the teacher and Stephen did too. When he sat down again his task was copying and he spent the time during this chatting and playing with his neighbour. After playtime the teacher explained to the class how to do some 'money' questions and Stephen listened. When the teacher had finished however she called Stephen over with his neighbour and explained to them again what they should do. Stephen then sat down and got on with his work, but with less enthusiasm, until dinnertime.

Stephen went to see the BSST teacher for his regular morning session on a Monday. The BSST sees children in a separate area. Because of space problems, the only place where the teacher can have her materials and any quiet is on a mezzanine floor which is also used as a general storage area and is rather claustrophobic. It is reached by a flight of steps from the infant area. The BSST is, however, able to keep a display of the work materials she uses with the children up there, as well as the children's work.

Stephen went off to the session quite happily after his class teacher had told him it was time to go. He went with his neighbour, Curtis, and there were just two of them in the group with the BSST teacher. The BSST teacher was using Fuzz Buzz workcards on which some words from the readers have to be put into sentences to complete them. The level of this work therefore corresponds with the work they do in class in their workbooks. Both children had to choose the right word to go in the sentences from a set of words, and they had to use shape (configuration), as well as testing that the sentence made sense. The teacher got them both to read and then look for the word that fitted. Stephen was very involved in this and seemed to be enjoying it. He was also keen to beat Curtis so rushed to put in a word once he had found it. He finished the session with the BSST at playtime and went naturally back in to the regular classroom after play.

Quantitative analysis

The coding of the observations showed that Stephen spent four-fifths (82 per cent) of his time working on basic skills work. The rest of the time he was either waiting for the teacher, fidgeting, or looking for materials. Over two-thirds of the work time was coded as full concentration, but this included the session with the support teacher. When he was in class, his concentration depended to some extent on what he was doing and how much the teacher was involved. So that in English, when he was working on his Fuzz Buzz workbook and reading to the teacher, he concentrated fully for 57 per cent of the time observed. However, two-thirds of that time the teacher was listening to him read or explaining what to do or checking his work.

Of the total classroom observation time, (seventy-five minutes excluding the withdrawal session) almost half involved Stephen having some kind of contact with his class teacher; some of this time he was waiting for her or talking to her about something else. But a third of Stephen's working time involved working individually with the teacher, and this was mostly in English. As long as she was with him, his concentration was sustained. Once she moved away or was distracted by another child, his concentration dropped: when the teacher was not with him two-thirds of his activity was coded as partial concentration. In maths, when working on his own without the teacher he spent a greater proportion of his work time concentrating well

(63 per cent). Stephen enjoyed maths and he listened hard in the class session while the teacher was explaining what to do.

In the session with the support teacher (not all of which was observed) Stephen worked with Curtis, and he concentrated well for 87 per cent of the time observed. For just a few minutes while Curtis was the focus of the teacher's attention, Stephen lost concentration and was less involved in what he was doing.

Comments

Stephen was popular with both the staff and the children. He was not disruptive of other children, and worked well as long as he was closely supervised, maths being an exception. When his class teacher was monitoring his progress closely he concentrated well and worked quietly. When she was with other children his concentration wandered. However, the teacher was able to organize her class effectively, giving them work to keep them busy, and she therefore had time to be with Stephen or the other five children with special needs. For a class teacher less able to keep the class occupied, it would have been more difficult for her to give Stephen such a lot of attention.

There was considerable overlap between the work Stephen did in the BSST sessions and in the class. Indeed much, though not all, of his reading/English classwork consisted of the practice work from the BSST session.

When Stephen was with the BSST his involvement with his work was very high. This was largely because of the high degree of attention from the BSST which kept him involved in the activity. For a child like Stephen, who was quiet but not very good at sustained concentration without fairly constant checking by his teacher, the class teacher's ability to organize the class is all important. In any individual sessions, or small groups, Stephen performed well and therefore, understandably, the class teacher would like him to see the BSST more often. This would certainly increase the time that he concentrates on his work. However, this is unlikely and so the bulk of his work will have to continue to be done in class, supervised by his class teacher.

His teacher worried about the amount of time she was spending with him, to the disadvantage of the middle band of children in the class, but while she was with him he concentrated on his work. The same was true of the time with the support teacher. Clearly while his concentration is sustained he does well and this class teacher seemed to have organized her class so that she could given Stephen the attention he needed while the rest of the class got on with their work.

Ben: Southshire

The target child, Ben, was in the third year of middle school (in a class of thiry-four). When we visited in December 1984 he was 10 years old. On the screening test in January 1982 he had an IQ of 103, a reading quotient of 90 and a maths Q of 98.

When he entered first school he was very over excited about contact with other children. He made very slow progress academically and by the second year was beginning to get into trouble in the playground and to become difficult. His teacher for the third year of first school described him as 'downright lazy' and 'made no effort'. She did not see him as an under-achiever, just 'a slow child'. In middle school he started to make progress but was still very weak — his concentration was poor, he had no confidence and a lack of drive — he did not seem to care whether he did well or not. His mother was regularly in the school then and discussed various ways of helping Ben. Eventually at the teacher's suggestion the parents got a tutor to give him some one-to-one attention. It was at the parents' insistence that Ben was finally referred to a remedial centre during his second year of middle school. By then he had a male teacher who admitted that he did not see Ben as a real problem because he was making progress. Spelling seemed to be the poorest skill and because of this very little writing got done. He still sometimes lied, cheated and stole but this was improving slowly.

Ben was going to the remedial centre for two whole afternoons a week: he walked there from school after dinner and his mother collected him from there at 3.30 p.m. He will continue to go to the centre for at least a year, until he goes to senior school. He was in a group of six boys, who worked individually on their tasks, rotating around the room and spending time with the teacher in turn to read to her and have their homework checked. The pattern of the session is to work for the first half of the afternoon and then to do some craft after play.

Ben's day

Ben started the session at the centre on the language master machine, listening to sounds (vowels) and writing them in his book. The next activity was a phonics work card, after three minutes he moved to a task which involved feeding cards through a Synchrofax machine, listening to the sounds produced and writing them down. Another work card followed: a picture of a boat and the writing 'b__t', he had to fill in the gaps. Then he did a Ginn 360 phonics work sheet — it was the wrong one, however, and he had to erase it and start again. When Ben had done all the tasks set by the teacher, he was allowed to read. Ben had kept at the tasks steadily, mostly with full concentration. He seemed, however, to be detached, unexcited, disinterested and, certainly, all the boys knew so exactly how to do all the tasks that it seemed as though they had done them many times before. Ben chose an exciting looking book which he then could not read. He flicked over the pages for a while but the teacher made him choose a simpler book and after a few minutes of this he seemed unutterably bored. His whole manner during these 'work' sessions was one of quiet disaffection. For a 10-year-old boy the tasks seemed very low level.

After play he made a Christmas card and at last he seemed slightly animated enjoying chatting and laughing with the other boys.

At school Ben's teachers did not know what he did at the remedial centre and there was no carry over of work. (He is, however, given homework from the remedial centre — an essay to write and reading to do). At school he joined in the class lessons. A class lesson in scripture held his attention for almost fifteen minutes until it came to having to write a short piece. After this it was domestic science: Ben made jelly fluff and then a finger puppet. During this he was animated and seemed to be enjoying himself. He had an argument with a girl but was able to take the problem to the teacher. He had to copy down the recipe for jelly fluff but seemed to have little trouble with this. The domestic science teacher did not find him a problem.

Quantitative analysis

In school, when Ben was at craft and scripture he spent 65 per cent of his time working. In scripture, which involved the class group he spent 80 per cent of his time fully concentrating on what the teacher was saying. During craft, when he worked much more on his own, he did not spend so much time concentrating fully on what he was doing (13 per cent).

At the remedial centre, the picture was rather different. Although he was in the small group with the teacher, he spent most of the time working on his own. He spent 77 per cent of his time at the centre working, and 59 per cent of this was full concentration on what he was doing. He had direct one to one contact with the remedial centre teacher for 38 per cent of his time at the centre, but only 25 per cent of this was coded as full concentration. Some of this time he was waiting for the teacher to check his work.

Comment

Ben seemed to be 'turned off' by school work. He had started as a lively excited boy at 5 but by 10 he was functioning rather like an automaton.

Somewhere along the line, something in the process of schooling (and an anxious mother) had managed to turn him off. For Ben, the remedial centre and school were quite separate activities. The level of activity at the remedial centre, the phonics, sound cards and so on, was much lower than that of the tasks he was supposed to do at school.

This was in complete contrast to a second target child, Donna. She had a lower IQ than Ben and went to a different centre, for two one-hour sessions per week. Donna was unusual in that her class teacher was the school's remedial expert and had been on a course at the remedial centre so she knew what to do with the practice work from the centre. (This was the only instance observed of remedial centre practice work being done in the class, so in a sense this child was not typical.) However, even so, when the class teacher did the practice work with Donna, this did not go well and Donna did not seem to enjoy it as she had at the centre. Although the gap in level of work is likely to increase as the children get older (Donna was 8 while Ben was 10) an important issue seems to be that Donna's teacher knew exactly what Donna did at the remedial centre and was familiar with the materials.

The help that Ben received at the remedial centre seemed potentially less beneficial than that which Donna received. Although Ben was there for longer he seemed unmotivated, not really enjoying it, and the work bore little relationship to what he did at school. Unfortunately, this was quite common in Southshire and is one of the undoubtedly negative points of this type of withdrawal. Futhermore, where a child goes to a remedial centre a danger is that the teacher may feel that little more need be done.

One reason why Southshire insists on keeping its remedial centres separate from schools is to remove the children from their scene of failure. For Ben, as far as his behaviour was concerned, this was certainly what happened. Donna too had a different persona at the remedial centre: she was chatty and lively in the small group in contrast to her quiet, shy role at school.

The children observed all seemed to enjoy going to the centres. They settled in and worked well. They appeared to enjoy the change, the individual attention and work which was not at 'frustration' level. With-drawal from the school to the centre did not seem to cause too much difficulty for the children we saw when they returned to the classroom. The length of time spent at the centre probably helped because it meant that they generally came back to school at a natural break. The contrast in atmosphere might, however, have been more noticeable to the children.

It is certainly much more of a 'withdrawal' than in Norborough, involving a bus, car or taxi journey to a remedial centre where they are joined by children from other schools. For all the target children except

Donna there was a complete absence of overlap between centre and class: the children might just as well have been to the dentist for all that the remedial centre activity impinged on their classroom activity.

Kim: Suburb

Kim attended a junior school of 350 children, in thirteen classes. The school is organized around a central courtyard; its catchment area is a housing estate, most of it Council-owned, but some owner-occupied. Kim was 8½-years-old and one of twenty-five children in one of the three second year junior classes. She transferred into the school from another junior school in the authority at the beginning of the school year. Her records showed that she had quite severe learning difficulties, particularly in reading and had been referred to the SPS in 1983 because of these and her very slow progress. She was assessed by the SPS who recommended reading help, and either part-time or full-time attendance at a remedial class. At the end of her last infant year when she was 7, her reading age on the Carver Reading Test (the LEA screening test) was 4.0 years.

Kim was described by her previous school as a pleasant child who tried hard and was anxious to please.

At the time of our visit, the school had no part-time teacher for remedial help, although it had had in the past, and all help was given by class teachers, either in class, or in sessions out of class while the Deputy Head took the rest of the class. Under this arrangement the class teacher took Kim, and another child Daniel, on their own for half-an-hour twice a week to help them on their special work and on other work they were having difficulties with. Usually she finished off the session with a game. Kim was using the Read, Write and Remember scheme and Oxford Junior Workbooks, as well as individual sheets for phonics, from the materials provided by the SPS teachers.

Kim's day

Kim was observed in her class for a morning, and in an individual session with her teacher while the Deputy took the class. In class, Kim sat at a desk in a group of four children, in the middle of the room. After registration, all children got out their maths books for practical maths, and the teacher reminded them about the work they had done with mirrors. She then handed out the mirrors as an introduction to a television programme which followed. The class went to a separate room and watched the fifteen-minute television programme and then went back to their classroom where they continued their maths and drew shapes they made with their mirrors in their books. The teacher went round to the children's desks to see how they were getting on and stopped to make sure Kim was getting a turn with the mirror. The class continued with this until play. Afterwards, it was assembly which the whole school attended. After assembly, Kim and Daniel were kept back to work alone with the class teacher while the rest went to music. In this session, the teacher heard Kim read the sounds and words from her worksheet and she read the words she had practised at home. When the rest of the class returned from music, they continued with their maths until dinnertime.

Kim sat quietly at her place during the class sessions. In maths, while the teacher was explaining what to do, she did not seem to be listening to the teacher, even when spoken to directly, but looked out of the window and into her desk. When the class went to watch television, however, she was quite involved and watched most of programme intently. After the programme Kim listened but without much enthusiasm while the teacher re-explained the practical maths task about mirrors. She took almost ten minutes to write the date in her book and to draw vertical lines to put the mirror on, so that in the maths session before playtime she got very little experience with the mirror. The teacher came over once to check that she was getting a turn and she had a go making a shape. Before she could draw it, it was playtime.

In the special session with the teacher and Daniel, doing some phonics Kim was still very quiet, and it was difficult to hear what she was saying. The teacher gave her lots of praise and encouragement ('good, that's the one, well done'). Kim leaned her head on her hand and said the sounds out very slowly. When she could not do it, or did not know the sound, she did not seem to try very hard and in the second half of the session the teacher had to push her to respond, by providing some of the sounds and asking questions. The teacher then explained what to do next and while the teacher listened to Daniel reading, Kim worked at her sound sheet ringing the rhyming words and then colouring a picture that made a rhyme. She got most pleasure from this colouring and spent time choosing which crayons to use. The session had to end when the class returned from music. The whole class restarted their maths work and Kim seemed to get more enjoyment from it this time. She chatted to her neighbour while they moved the mirror over the paper and she drew the shapes quite happily in her book until it was time to stop for dinner. This work was quite within her capabilities, but she took a long time to do the drawings. Apart from the television programme, this was her most animated session, she was otherwise a quiet, rather dreamy girl who sat in her place and caused little bother.

Quantitative analysis

Kim spent 73 per cent of the observation time working and nearly half of this was full concentration. Kim spent nearly half of the observation period with her teacher in the small special group, when the rest of the class were at music; most of her full concentration (65 per cent) was therefore during this session. However, although she *could* concentrate well with the teacher, she spent an equal amount of time only partially concentrating. This included time she spent interacting directly with the teacher as well as when the teacher was listening to Daniel read. In maths, Kim's concentration was almost all coded as partial (67 per cent), except during the television programme when she concentrated fully for 40 per cent of her time. In the class sessions after television and before dinnertime, although she was quite enjoying what she was doing, she chatted to her neighbour at the same time and her concentration on the task was only partial. Kim spent over a quarter of her time (29 per cent) 'drifting', staring into space, but not fidgeting.

Comment

Kim did not do her individual work with the phonic sheets from the reading programme during class sessions. Her teacher thought the work was rather boring, since Kim easily lost interest, and that it would have been a waste of time to spend whole class sessions doing the work. During class sessions therefore Kim did the same work as the rest of the class although she found this hard and did need prompting to get on. In English, which was not observed, the children all worked at their own level, and Kim worked in her Oxford workbook or on her Read, Write and Remember exercises. The teacher also considered that the photocopied reading sheets were not very pleasant to work with and made Kim's work noticeably different from the rest of the class. Because the Deputy Head took the class for some sessions, for example music, Kim's teacher had time to spend with her going through the reading programme. It is possible, however, that Kim would have enjoyed the music session more than the session with the class teacher.

The class teacher maintained that she would have found it difficult to fit in Kim's special work any other way because the sessions at the school were all only half an hour long, and this meant that usually she had to spend half of that time getting the class organized and answering children's queries. As the description showed, although the children were doing maths work, they restarted the *same* task three times. Fitting Kim's individual work into this would certainly have taken up time.

Kim did not seem to benefit particularly from the withdrawal session with her class teacher to any great extent, and she seemed disinterested in the work. Like other children we have described, however, Kim did concentrate better when the teacher was with her. As the description of Kim's class shows, giving sufficient attention to the children on individual programmes can be difficult for teachers, even when there is help available from someone else in the school. Gregg, a target child in another school in this LEA, got a good deal of attention in class and from the Deputy Head in his withdrawal session. Kim got far less attention from her class teacher in class, partly because of the way that the class was organized, with the special needs children spread across the room at different tables, so that the teacher could only help one of them at a time, and partly because of the short sessions. This meant that Kim's teacher had to keep restarting the class on their work. Kim's special work with the loose sheets of sound matching, blending and so on, was only done in the withdrawal sessions. As the session with Kim showed, she did not concentrate particularly well even then (one of the very few target children not to concentrate well in a small group session) and so leaving her to get on in class would probably have been unsuccessful.

Without a high degree of input from their teachers none of the target children in Suburb seemed to work hard on the materials, and it is possible that they found them rather uninspiring to work on; several of the children spent a high proportion of this time on the special materials just colouring-in.

Sheena: Ruralshire

The target child in Ruralshire, Sheena, was in a primary school of 216 children which had both a 0.5 remedial teacher on the staff and a visiting PRT (0.3) from the new support service, the Learning Difficulty Support Service (LDSS). The school was in a deprived housing estate outside a seaside resort town.

Sheena was 8 years old, and in the first year junior class of thirty-one children. She was described in her infant records as a solitary child who needed a lot of attention and encouragement; her reading was slow and she could not concentrate for long. There were family problems and Sheena was on the 'At Risk' register. She was eager to please, however, and tried hard. During the spring term she had spent a month in a children's home and this had greatly disturbed her.

When we visited in January 1985 her test scores were: Neale Reading Analysis — below 5 years 8 months, comprehension — no score; Young's Group Reading Test — below seventy. She had started in the school's remedial group in her last infant year.

In Sheena's classroom the children were grouped by reading and English ability. There were two tables of 'good', two of 'middle' and two-

and-a-half of 'poor' children. Out of a class of thirty-one, fourteen were classified by the teacher as needing special help and all attended the school remedial group. Sheena sat with a boy called Keith who was also very slow, and she was considered a stabilizing influence on him. They sat away from the other children, but not particularly near the teacher's desk.

Sheena was going two or three mornings a week for half-an-hour to the school's 0.5 remedial teacher. This remedial teacher and the visiting PRT often worked as a team, the PRT devising work schedules and testing the children while the remedial teacher heard the children read and did practice work. A blue exercise book in which the children do their work in the remedial session is sent with the child from the remedial to class teacher.

Sheena's day

Sheena went to her remedial session at 9.10 a.m. soon after arriving at school. There were four children and the part-time teacher together in the 'remedial room'. The children were doing work cards and taking it in turn to read to the teacher. Sheena started off with a work card which involved copying a short sentence and colouring a drawing. The sentences were taken from the Fuzz Buzz books which Sheena was reading and she wrote in an exercise book which she later showed to her class teacher. She worked hard on this task and was not distracted by what was going on in the room, resisting attempts by a neighbour to help her. This was a task which she could do without too much difficulty and she enjoyed it. After a little more than ten minutes it was her turn to read to the teacher. She would not sit down next to the teacher nor follow the line with her finger, but read without too much stumbling or hesitation. She read for almost ten minutes including one interruption. The teacher was pleased with her and said that she would tell the class teacher to hear her read these pages. Sheena then went back to her work cards and chose the right colours by reading the sentence; again she concentrated well.

During the withdrawal session, before reading to the teacher and while sharpening her crayons Sheena chatted easily to the teacher and initiated much of the discussion herself. As far as her work was concerned she gave the impression of a child who was self-contained and involved.

When Sheena went back in to the classroom the other children were all doing silent reading, taking it in turns to read to the teacher so Sheena did not have to slot into a lesson. However, Sheena started by reading a library book which was too hard for her: she flicked through the pages looking at the pictures and only concentrating part of the time. Soon she was asked to go and read to the class teacher — she took her Fuzz Buzz books and exercise book and told the teacher what she had been doing in the remedial session. Sheena read to him (happily running her finger along the line) and they talked for about five minutes. Because they talked about her work in the withdrawal session Sheena was with the teacher for slightly longer than the other children in the class. Sheena went back to sit down and practice her reading with her Fuzz Buzz book and her wordbook. However, she had been at the same activity, basically, all morning and it was now nearly playtime: she fidgeted, gazed around, lay with her head on her book and generally gave the impression of being bored. For a short while she chatted to her neighbour, Keith, and read her words to him, until the teacher called to the neighbour to get on. Then Sheena gave up any further attempt to work for the few minutes until playtime: she brushed her hair and gazed out of the window.

In the afternoon the class, supervised by a student teacher, was doing a project on food. The group of poor readers sat with the student teacher while the rest of the class finished some other work; the student teacher explained to these children what to do. They had a sheet each with eight food words on it. They read the words together and then they went away and drew each one and wrote some sentences using the words. The class teacher was also in the room and twice when Sheena was writing about the food she got stuck on a word and went to him with her dictionary book for help. Once when the class teacher was busy and did not notice Sheena she just walked back to her seat, making no attempt to catch his attention or interrupt him. At her table she chatted and messed about with her neighbour, Keith, except when she copied down a word from her dictionary or the board — when she concentrated for a short period.

Sheena was much less likely to initiate contact with her class teacher than she had with the remedial teacher. Consequently she did only a limited amount of work in the class project lesson.

Quantitative analysis

Sheena seemed much more like the children described by Croll and Moses as slow learners than some of the other children described in this chapter. She spent 66 per cent of her time working, mostly on basic skills (some of the work was her food project) but she also spent 21 per cent of the observation period fidgeting. When she was working, she concentrated fully on her work for only 49 per cent of the time; most of her concentrated activity came in the withdrawal group (65 per cent), with the school remedial teacher. She concentrated well in this group, better than in class. Not much of this was actual one-to-one contact; Sheena was working on her workcard within the group, and the remedial teacher was nearby. Her one-to-one contact with the remedial teacher (13 per cent of her time in the group) was while she read to her.

In total, 19 per cent of Sheena's time involved contact with a teacher, and half of this was really just organizing talk, asking to sharpen pencils and so on. Two-thirds of this teacher contact occurred in the withdrawal group, with the remedial teacher when also Sheena was more forthcoming than in class. So in class, on our visit, Sheena had little individual attention from her teacher, except when reading. He did, however, talk to her quite a lot about what she had done in the withdrawal group.

Comment

Because of the way that help is provided in Ruralshire, there was variation in the way schools responded to their children's needs. Most of the target children did, however, go to some form of withdrawal group, whether this was taught by the PRT from the support service or by the school remedial teacher. Sheena was therefore not unlike other target children in terms of the help she got. She received individual attention in the withdrawal session and also did follow-up work with her class teacher in the classroom, ie, using the same reading scheme and work cards. In the classroom however, she gave up easily and did not concentrate on what she was doing. In the small group she not only concentrated more but was more forthcoming which meant that she was never 'stuck'. By contrast, in class the high level of fidgeting observed was clearly due to an inappropriate level of work and poor supervision. Sheena only concentrated fully when she knew exactly what to do, how to do it, and was able to do it. Any work that was slightly harder than this needed more individual adult attention than she was able to get in class. Her working style and willingness to enter into communication with the adults were very different in the withdrawal session and the class session. For these reasons if the small withdrawal sessions were to cease and no changes were made in the organization of Sheena's classroom, she would be engaged in even less educational activity than currently.

Wayne: Newtown

Wayne, the target child, was a second year junior in a school of 240, in an area of pre-war private housing. There were two special needs coordinators in the school, one for the upper juniors and one for the lower. There were few Asian children at the school which made it unusual compared with most of the other schools visited in the LEA, although a teacher came from the minority group support service to take six children once a week. There was a part-time teacher (0.3) who came into school but did not do remedial work, and both the coordinators were full-time class teachers. This school was chosen to illustrate how the system worked in Newtown without extra staffing (either part-timers or from Section Eleven money), and where the class teacher had to deal with the children on individual programmes without the extra support that was available elsewhere.

Wayne was 8 years 4 months old, and in a second year junior class of twenty-nine children. He was one of two children the class teacher was working with on programmes, and at the time of the visit was working on a spelling programme. Wayne's score on the Salford Sentence Reading test at the end of the first year, when he was 8 years old, was 6 years 4 months (standard score seventy-nine). Wayne's record showed that since 1979 he had been referred to both the speech therapist and the educational psychologist because he had very poor expressive language. He was described on the referral form as non-communicative and withdrawn, as well as making little progress academically. He was put on to the Ginn 360 Reading Scheme and the EPs also suggested the LEA's special programmes to help in specific areas.

Wayne's day

All the observations of Wayne took place in the classroom, during which time he did some work on his programme. He sat at a table with a group of other children. The teacher went round from group to group and consequently there was no queuing to see him at his desk. On the day of our visit there was a mother helping in the classroom and a student teacher on placement.

The first session was maths. At Wayne's table they were doing time and clocks, filling in the answers on sheets. The rest of the class then stopped doing this and moved on to some other maths work. Wayne's group, however, continued with this topic. To start off with Wayne was not particularly involved and listened instead to what the teacher was saying to the parent sitting at his table. When the teacher went off, Wayne was drawn into the group by the parent asking him questions about time. He responded to these questions but did not always get the answer right and she asked him again. He looked very blank on a couple of occasions, particularly about quarter hours and after ten minutes seemed rather tired. After helping him, the mother moved to help another child at the same table and Wayne had to get on with sums, which were straightforward additions (5 + 3, 8 + 2). He had the abacus to help him and the clock to time how long it took him. He worked well at this for about four minutes, during which time the teacher walked over to look, raised his eyebrows and smiled at Wayne and went away again. When he stopped working, he gazed round the room and the teacher came over to see if he had finished. He set Wayne a new task and Wayne got going again. After a few minutes he lost interest again and the teacher went to check how he was doing. He then started off on the new task again and worked through it oblivious to the rest of the class packing up around him, although the teacher went over to him twice during this time.

After playtime, the children started on language work, with different groups working at different levels. Some children were doing comprehension (using the Ginn 360 Scheme) some phonics and some spelling; the slow group was doing spelling. The teacher started Wayne off on the Synchrofax machine with headphones on. He pushed the word cards through the machine and listened to the words. As he listened, other children came up and distracted him and wanted to listen too, and after this he lost concentration and pushed the cards through absent-mindedly. The teacher went back to check that he had done them and Wayne read him the kwywords. Then Wayne waited while the teacher explained to the student what to do with Wayne's spelling sheet, and he went to get his word book when asked.

Wayne then went with the student teacher to do his reading programme. This involved reading the new words in his Ginn 360 book, which were corrected when he made a mistake. There were six steps in the programme, starting with learning the first five words and ending with spelling correctly all twenty words in a test situation. He completed the test for the previous words in forty-three seconds, and his class teacher praised him for doing well. Wayne and the student teacher then went through the next set of words. He spelt the words out, and then tested himself by writing them down. He seemed to be involved in the task. After five minutes or so, he took one of his language cards back to the machine and put the headphones on. Almost immediately a child went up and distracted him but was called away by the teacher. He finished listening to the words and went back to his place. He then went over to the teacher, for the first time, and asked if he could go out because he felt sick. He came back five minutes later saying that he was better and had not been sick. His teacher suggested that there was too much work; they both grinned and Wayne put his programme sheet on the teacher's desk and went off to dinner.

Wayne worked well in short bursts and then lost interest; usually his teacher noticed and came over to ask how he was getting on, but there was very little extended contact with his class teacher.

Quantitative analysis

Wayne spent 72 per cent of the observation time working on the basic skills, all at his own level. More than half of his work time was full concentration (56 per cent), although he concentrated better on his own, than when the mother who was helping out was with him. In language work, after play Wayne concentrated fully for 63 per cent of the time, but some of this was spent with the student teacher. Wayne only spent 23 per cent of his time in contact with his class teacher over the whole period and little of this (28 per cent) was in full concentration.

Comment

For Wayne, the individual work he did as part of his individual programme did not stand out from the work other children were doing because they were all working at different levels on various schemes. In a more formal classroom setting his programme would not have fitted in so well and he might have been more conspicuous. Neither did it involve the class teacher in spending a great deal of time with him, although of course on our visit there was a mother and a student teacher in the class. However, even when the student tested Wayne on his words it did not take longer than five minutes, which would not have been difficult for the class teacher to have managed. The teacher did, however, have to prepare Wayne's programme, ie develop the steps which he had to learn and be tested on, and this obviously took time.

The teacher was on the move most of the time, not waiting for problems to come to him, which made it easier for him to check on Wayne's progress on his regular perambulations around the room. Unlike the children in Suburb working on their individual programmes, Wayne did not have much contact with his teacher and was able to work well with just this prompting. Wayne's contact with his class teacher did not always involve verbal interaction but may have been just a smile or nod from the teacher. The low level of contact enabled the class teacher to go round the class seeing other children and return to Wayne when necessary, rather than remaining with Wayne to keep him working and going to other children only when crises arose. The class teacher's organization of his class seemed crucial. Interestingly the teacher of the other target child (Mark) observed in that school but in another class, had organized her class so that she could be with other children and still see what Mark was doing. If he was not working she did not go over but just called his name which set him back at work. She did, however, spend more time with him than Wayne's did with him, because she spent time at the beginning of the session sorting out his work and getting him involved.

In Newtown, there was a variety of organization in different schools which meant that some children did their special programmes in withdrawal sessions. Wayne remained in his classroom and did his special work there, as part of his normal curriculum. This is how the system is supposed to operate but was comparatively rare in the schools we visited. As we explained in the previous chapter many of the teachers in Newtown had not really internalized this approach and saw the individual programmes of work as something 'extra', perhaps even in addition to the normal curriculum.

Peter: Midshire

Peter, the target child, was at a primary school which was making arrangements to meet special needs both through the use of central teams and from within its own resources. The school, in a town on the edge of the county, had a catchment area of mixed housing — some poor quality Council housing and some semi-detached private housing. It was relatively new and open plan. There were 430 pupils on roll and there were members of the central team for disaffected pupils coming into the school for a fourth year child; a teacher of the deaf; a member of the E2L team for a Chinese boy; an outreach teacher supporting a child returned to mainstream from a unit and providing general advice; and a part-time teacher taking four children for help by withdrawal, who was allocated termly via the Area Coordinator.

Peter was in a second year junior class of thirty-four, and was one of twelve children the class teacher thought had special needs, including a boy being reintegrated into mainstream schooling. Peter was 8 years 10 months old at the time of observation. He was rather a solitary child whom the school considered was seriously underachieving. In 1984 when he was 7 years 7 months old his reading age on the Southgate Test was 7 years and the previous year his score on the Schonell was 5 years 4 months. The records showed that he had difficulty knowing left from right, problems with letter formation, and problems of motor coordination. His overall record described him as 'poor' in most areas although of average ability. He was referred to the SPS in February of the school year of our visit because of these difficulties and because of behaviour problems. There was a suggestion that he might be hyperactive and at the time of our visit his mother was trying him on an orange squash-free diet.

He had four sessions of twenty minutes each week with the visiting remedial teacher who came to the school, and had been having this help for four months. The visiting teacher said that he had made progress in this time but tended to be distractible. His class teacher also thought he had made progress, but found he needed considerable individual attention in class if he was to get the work done. He also used some materials provided by the outreach teacher. Peter was chosen as the child to be described for Midshire, rather than a child receiving help from the new special needs team of LDTs, since the latter service is intended for children who are likely to require a statement.

Peter's day

Peter was observed during his session with the remedial teacher and in his classroom area. He was a quiet child, and gave little sign of the hyperactivity suggested in his records.

The session with the remedial teacher took place first thing in the morning in a small room off the lower juniors classroom area. He started off the session doing 'time'. The teacher asked questions about time, using a clock face with movable hands, and Peter answered verbally or drew the answer on a sheet of clock faces the teacher had prepared. This work was part of what the class teacher had asked the remedial teacher to do with him. After five minutes of this, during which he concentrated well and responded to all the questions, the teacher switched to some sound puzzles. He had to put the letters together to make a word shown by a picture, in this case, the words all ended in 'y', 'happy, holly, hilly, dolly, penny' and so on. Again he concentrated well on doing this task, which he got right most times, although he mixed up 'b' and 'd'. He talked about the pictures and the teacher asked him about the words and kept up a flow of talk. This lasted for five minutes and then for the last half of the session he was allowed to do a dot-to-dot picture. The teacher made sure he included all the numbers and then they said the numbers out loud as he got to each one. All the teacher's conversation, which was almost constant, was related to the work and included praise for good work. When he had completed the picture and identified it, it was the end of the session. He got up and went back to his classroom on his own.

The rest of his class were doing drama, and by the time he had found them it was too late for him to join in properly so he hung around until his class teacher sent him back to the class area to read to the end of the session.

The observation continued after playtime. The children in the class were in groups, some of which were making calendars, working out the dates and so on, where the teacher was explaining what to do. Two groups of children were doing practical maths, weighing and measuring and mirrors. Peter was with several other children in a group doing art and craft. His class teacher felt that after his intensive session in the morning he should not do anything more 'special' and art offered an opportunity for him to practice his motor skills. He spent his time during the session colouring in animals with wax crayons. He was absorbed in what he was doing and sang to himself. He did not take any notice of the other children until they addressed him. He then chatted to one of them while he cut out the elephant he had been colouring. The teacher came over once or twice to see how he was getting on; he told her that the elephant he was cutting out was the fourth one, and continued cutting. He wandered to and fro while doing this seeing what the others were doing and seemed to be chatting, but to nobody in particular. When he finished cutting out he stuck the animals down on to a large piece of paper. The teacher then gathered up the children in the art group and showed them some books about animals. Peter did not seem particularly interested in the books. He stared vaguely out of the window until the teacher asked him a question and then showed him some flash cards which he read with few errors. She listened to him read the words once and then sent him back to his glueing and cutting out. He took no notice when the teacher told the class to pack away and continued until the teacher went over and told him individually to stop. Then he did stop, put the glue away and joined the rest of the class for a story, sitting on the floor.

Peter was also observed in class the next day, again he spent a good deal of his morning doing art work, but also had a short session with his class teacher, reading his flashcards, which had been provided at the suggestion of the outreach teacher. The rest of the class did practical maths. The teacher asked Peter the sounds on the cards and he said them and then wrote them down. He did not appear involved in the task and the teacher simply asked him the word and then went on to the next. After a few minutes the teacher gave him a card with some sums on and told him to get on with them and she left him while she went to check other children. Peter stood at the table and did the sums and then took them over to his teacher who checked them. He got them all right and the teacher praised him. He asked her if he could do what he wanted next and she said he could. He wandered off to watch one group of children working with magnets. After a few moments, he wandered back to his picture and stuck another leaf, which he had made earlier, on the tree he had drawn. He then went over to play with some Lego. He lay on the floor, making a Lego aeroplane and played with this until it was time to clear away for dinner.

Quantitative analysis

Peter spent 78 per cent of the observation time working, but in class, ie, apart from the session with the remedial teacher, he spent only 31 per cent of his time on basic skills work. The rest of his time he was doing art or playing. In the session with the remedial teacher he spent 100 per cent of his time working on language and number work, which included games. He also worked for the whole session, so that it was only in class that he spent time off task.

Peter concentrated well; 68 per cent of his work time was coded as full concentration. He was absorbed in his art work and concentrated fully on it for three-quarters of the time he was doing it. He did not seem particularly involved in his brief sessions with the class teacher and only 9 per cent of these two sessions was coded as full concentration. Like most of the other children described, Peter concentrated well in his individual session with the remedial teacher (93 per cent of the time).

Altogether, 47 per cent of the observation involved Peter in contact with a teacher, 54 per cent of his contact was in the withdrawal session and only 22 per cent of the contacts involved Peter in work-related interaction with his class teacher, the rest was general questions about what to do and instructions to clear away.

Comment

Peter was a rather strange and solitary child, who seemed to be very much in a world of his own. In his session with the remedial teacher, he was still quiet, but more forthcoming about himself than in the classroom where he had little to say to his class teacher. The session with the remedial teacher went well: this teacher had an easy manner with all the children. Peter seemed to enjoy the work and responded well to questions. The teacher kept up a flow of conversation about the work which may have helped to maintain Peter's concentration. Although the teacher was doing some maths work with him, requested by the class teacher, there was no actual carry over of work from the session to the classroom; the remedial teacher brought her own materials, which Peter did not use in the classroom. There was little time for liaison between the remedial teacher and the class teacher, and the class teacher was not happy with the way Peter came back to class in the middle of the drama session.

The class teacher did do some work on language, reading and number with Peter but her manner was very different from the remedial teacher's. When she was asking Peter the words on the flash cards, she just showed him the cards and waited for his response. Peter did not seem interested in the words in the way he had been in the individual session. The teacher did not like some of the materials she received, particularly loose sheets, and tended not to use them.

The class was large and had a high proportion (a third) of children whom the teacher considered had special needs. Peter liked art and concentrated well, unlike maths, so that the teacher could leave him to do this while she attended to other children. She also considered that the effort he put in during his individual session meant that he should not be pushed into more special work during class. The teacher of a first year child observed at the school who also saw the remedial teacher, felt the same way too. However, this meant that apart from art, Peter was unlikely to be doing the same work as the rest of the class, particularly in basic skills. It should be said that the emphasis on art and play here was a reflection of the head teacher's philosophy that children, and particularly children with special needs, still needed opportunities to play in class in order to develop.

The overall picture of Peter and of the school, despite the new developments in the LEA and the increased help they had in school, is little different from a traditional withdrawal model with little classroom carry over. This was generally how the system of help was working in Midshire, although SNAP had been introduced to schools together with other in-service programmes.

Overview

To answer the questions posed at the beginning of the chapter, the children worked for between half and three-quarters of their time and this was virtually all basic skills work. This finding is very similar to that reported by Croll and Moses (1985). In general therefore, children worked, ie, were on task, for the majority of their time. The proportion of time spent fidgeting was lower than might have been expected, although this may have been a feature of the children described here, since several of them were rather quiet. Other children we observed were not so hardworking — spending as much as 25 per cent of their time fidgeting.

Arrangements for class teaching, not surprisingly, varied from place to place and are discussed in more detail below. Teachers differed in whether they grouped all children with special needs together or spread them out between groups. In some cases, these children were seated very near to the class teacher's desk. For most of the children there were times when the class would be divided into groups working at different tasks and/or levels and the target children could slot into this quite well. Where it was difficult for children to cope was in very formal class settings — rows of desks for example — or class lessons, although this was very much the exception.

The amount of curriculum overlap between what the children were doing and what the rest of the class were doing varied from LEA to LEA, but generally it would be fair to say that the children we observed with special needs were regularly doing separate work at a different level from the rest of their class. This was more noticeable in places where children were on individual teaching programmes, than where withdrawal occurred. Where children were doing the same work as their peers, however, they were often unable to maintain their concentration for long.

Most strikingly, however, all the children bar one — Wayne (Newtown) — received a considerable amount of teacher attention and time. It is difficult to know how representative this was and presumably it was partly affected by our presence, but by and large where small groups were timetabled, the level of contact probably reflected the normal pattern. For many children who were withdrawn, the major proportion of the teacher attention and contact they received occurred outside the classroom in these withdrawal sessions. An example of this would be Peter (Midshire), who had a high level of individual teacher contact in his withdrawal session but little contact in the classroom. At the other end of the scale Stephen (Norborough) when we observed him had high levels of teacher contact in the classroom as well as in the withdrawal session.

Moving from one setting to the other, ie from withdrawal group to classroom, also varied. In some cases, for instance for Donna in Southshire, return to school was at a natural break, such as playtime. Sheena returned to a quiet reading session and could easily join in but Peter, in the observed session returned to drama, and could not easily join in. This did not always happen, but it illustrates the serious difficulties of leaving a child to wander back and forth with little liaison between class teacher and remedial teacher. In Kim's case, she was excluded from music, rather than withdrawn, in order to have a session with the teacher. Although she did concentrate during this session it seems unfortunate to have missed out on a fairly rare topic like music rather than something like maths, which happened every day. However, there were additional difficulties at Kim's school due to the very short sessions, which made it difficult for the teacher to fit in individual teaching.

Individual attention from the teacher resulted, not surprisingly, in better levels of concentration from the children and a greater involvement in their work. Some children *only* concentrated on their work if the teacher was with them; as soon as she turned away to attend to someone else, the child's attention wandered and their concentration dropped. If children are working alone through individual programmes and their teachers are aware of the need for constant supervision this of course presents something of a difficulty for the teacher, and explains their feelings of having no time for other children in the class. Some children did not need the teacher to be with them all the time (for example, Wayne — Newtown) but did need monitoring or encouragement from the teacher to keep working, and this demanded a specific type of classroom organization.

Moving to more general issues, as far as the children are concerned, the six LEAs break down into two groups: those which offer help via withdrawal and those which offer help via individual teaching programmes in the classroom. For both these groups there is a range of provision, so that withdrawal can vary from a situation where the work is only done outside the classroom in a group or one to one, for example Ben, to a situation where work is carried over, back into the classroom, for example Donna (both from Southshire). Teaching programmes can vary too, so that in Suburb, the programmes were made up of materials produced by the specialist teachers and in Newtown, the programmes were developed by the child's own class teacher, using the child's own competence and curriculum as a guide. To some extent, Stephen, a target child in Norborough, crosses the boundary between withdrawal and individual teaching programmes, since he got both.

While the teacher contact levels were, on the whole, high, and the children concentrated well during this contact, there are some important differences between withdrawal and teaching programmes. These led to differences in the types of contact and the children's behaviour, in withdrawal sessions compared with class teaching which seemed to be due to a change of scene, to high levels of adult interest and contact, and work at a level where the children could succeed rather than fail. In the withdrawal sessions where children were seeing another teacher, either outside school or in school, the children were generally much more forthcoming than with their teacher in the classroom. This was true for both the Southshire children, Donna and Ben, who both went to remedial centres. However, the same effect was also noticeable in small groups within school, for example Sheena, and is one of the benefits cited by class teachers of withdrawal.

In small groups the children also seemed much more involved in their work, probably because of the level of teacher interest and supervision. For example Sheena (Ruralshire) did not concentrate well on her project work in the classroom and got more out of her withdrawal session. Of course, this may have been partly to do with the fact that her class teacher knew that she was going to the remedial teacher regularly and therefore left her to get on with it, while he attended to other children. However, one child, Kim (Suburb) did not show a higher level of interest in her work in withdrawal sessions that she did in class and one possible reason for this is that the work was boring. Another reason for disinterest could be to do with the person doing the session. Kim was the only one of the children we describe withdrawn by her class teacher: maybe one of the reasons why children were more forthcoming and involved in their withdrawal sessions is as much because of the change in person as the change in work.

The issue of individual teaching programmes is complex. As we pointed out in chapter 5, and as these descriptions show, there may sometimes be little difference for the child between being on an individual programme and being withdrawn. In Newtown, some teachers using the programme worked using withdrawal. Wayne, however, demonstrated a rather different experience of a teaching programme. Rather than having either a high degree of class teacher attention or special withdrawal, Wayne worked on his individual programme with a minimum of teacher attention. This we must assume is how Newtown's individual teaching programmes are meant to operate, in which case we have much to learn from the organization of Wayne's classroom.

In discussing Wayne earlier, it was pointed out that Wayne's teacher had organized his classroom so that Wayne's individual work did not stand out from what other children were doing, because all the children were working individually, or in groups. Wayne also had work that he could do on his own, as long as he was regularly encouraged by his teacher. Wayne's teacher moved around the room checking children's work rather than sitting at his desk, operating a queue system. His approach made it possible for him to provide the brief encouragement to Wayne when it was needed rather than Wayne standing waiting to see him. It is likely that teachers would get more time to see children in the middle band, about whom they are always concerned, if they circulated in the classroom, rather than waiting for problems to come to them. This was, of course, a recommendation of the 1978 *HMI Primary Survey* (DES, 1978b) and our study shows it is still important.

To answer now our first general question, 'what is it like for a child receiving special help', it is a truism that every child's experience is different. Nevertheless, we described, for many of the children, two types of education. In one, they are the focus of attention and are given a lot of praise and encouragement. In the other, they have to get on as best they could within the class. This happens with 'traditional' withdrawal but also when children are withdrawn for individual teaching programmes. In some cases this may mean that children do very little 'work' when they are in their classrooms.

We have described only six children from our case study LEAs and these descriptions represent only some of the ways that provision works in those LEAs. Nevertheless, we have identified various features of the provision available which undoubtedly affect children's experience of it.

We have aimed to describe the experience of 'typical' remedial children. As their histories show we have described children with a range of difficulties: timidity, poor language development, family problems and so on. Thus, although our overall focus is on what might be considered a restricted range of children, the children's problems described here were anything but narrow. To reiterate what we said at the beginning of this chapter: they are typical of the children primary teachers deal with every day in perfectly ordinary classrooms. We hope that by identifying some good and poor elements of different models of support, we can attempt to suggest ways in which teachers can more easily help these children. This is our aim in the next chapter when, among other things, we take up the thorny issue of what constitutes the best deal for the child.

Notes

1 Details of the observation method are available from the authors at the Institute of Education, 20 Bedford Way, London WC1H 0AL (Screening and Special Educational Provision in Schools Project, Final Report to ESRC April 1986).
2 There is of course plenty of evidence that teachers behave differently to boys and girls in the classroom.

Chapter 9

Conclusions

Summary

We start by summarizing the main points from each of the earlier chapters.

The literature reviewed in the first chapter suggested that there seems to be no consensus about the best way to provide help, particularly with reading, for children who have difficulties in learning. Nevertheless, moves within remedial/special education indicated a direction for change that seems to have been followed in the wake of the Warnock Report. This move can be summed up as supporting the child within the ordinary classroom via the class teacher. The philosophy behind many of the new developments is that in order to reach the failing learner it is necessary to involve the class teacher, building up her expertise and confidence. The aim is not to deskill the teacher by centralizing expertise, but to foster expertise in the class teacher herself, and the early Rutter work demonstrated the effectiveness of this approach (Rutter, Tizard and Whitmore, 1970).

Traditionally, standardized reading tests have been used to identify children in need of further help although more recently checklists have increased in popularity, particularly at the younger age group. LEA policy in identification, as disclosed via our questionnaire survey, is generally to have some form of screening programme. Usually these testing programmes take place at more than one age and typically involve transfer points, infants to junior, and junior to secondary. Reading tests are the most popular, as is taking a cut-off point to determine which children shall be seen, ie children scoring below a certain score would automatically be considered for extra help. Where checklists are used, these tend to be developed within the LEA and in some cases form part of in-service training. It is rare for LEAs to evaluate their screening procedures. No doubt this is partly to do with the difficulties outlined in chapter 2 regarding evaluation but also because of the way that screening is regarded, that is very much as a current indicator and not as a 'predictive' activity.

The teachers in our case study schools were unlikely to rely on test scores alone when identifying children who needed special help. In LEAs where there was a screening programme teachers were more likely to use test scores, both from the screening test and other tests. However in all six LEAs, teachers combined test scores with their own judgment and records of children's progress to decide whether children needed special help. It is therefore unlikely that children would be put forward for help as a result of the screening programme alone.

In terms of the type of provision made for these children, local authorities typically have some form of a remedial/special needs support and advisory service, in addition to any part-time staffing which schools may have. The size of these services varies but, generally, they do not reach a very large number of the children needing help. Changes suggested in the Warnock Report, of unifying the range of services and providing support in the form of advice to class teachers rather than direct teaching, have been taking place in LEAs. The change, as we suggested earlier, has been partly because of the Warnock Report, partly because of dissatisfaction with current practices and also, originally, as part of a drive to reduce expenditure. Cuts in spending had meant staff reductions in some LEAs and this had helped in the move from teaching to advisory services. However, particularly since 1982, LEAs were more likely to have increased the number of support staff, especially of educational psychologists. Despite the move to advisory and support services, withdrawal of children from class (and school) was still widespread at the time of our questionnaire.

The case studies illustrated a range of forms of provision. Norborough has developed a new support service of teachers who offer materials and teach; Southshire has a well-established system of helping children with specific reading difficulties through withdrawal to centres; Suburb's reading programme has been running for some time and forms the backbone of a system of classroom-based support; Ruralshire was just beginning to develop new teams of advisory teachers who had started working in part of the LEA. (The new service was only just getting started due to earlier financial constraints which had also resulted in the ending of the screening programme.) In Newtown, there has been rapid and wholescale change to provide support to the class teacher, who has to take responsibility for children with special needs, through in-service training and individual teaching programmes; Midshire has set up a wide range of new developments, designed to meet a similarly wide range of children's needs.

Each of these LEAs represented different models of support and therefore different experiences for the class teacher and the child, as well as for the support services themselves. As the brief descriptions of the situation in each of the six case study LEAs show, these changes or developments in the support services have not always gone smoothly.

The teachers' responses to our short questionnaire showed that the class teachers in most of our case study LEAs were not entirely happy with the help provided by their LEA. The reasons for dissatisfaction varied from one LEA to another depending on the setting, type and amount of provision, as well as messages received from the LEA: not enough help in Ruralshire, not enough help to certain groups of children in Southshire; disappointment at the loss of schools' own part-time staff in Norborough and Midshire, and the time needed to organise children on individual programmes of work in Newtown or Suburb.

Teachers' feelings about the help they received did not necessarily relate to the size of their class, or number of children with special needs. Teacher satisfaction was related in part to the match between what they considered good ways of helping children with special needs, and what was available in their LEA. Where the two coincided, for example Suburb and Newtown, the level of satisfaction was higher than elsewhere. The desire for smaller classes and more withdrawal-type help was widespread but, significantly, was much less pronounced in some LEAs than others. The popularity of withdrawal showed up in the continuing use of this method even with individual teaching programmes. This illustrated one sort of mismatch between the LEA view of how a programme should work and how it was perceived and used by teachers.

Teachers' feelings of dissatisfaction are bound to have an effect on the way a service works. It seems that the presentation of new developments is a key issue here, particularly where services are changing rapidly. In Norborough for instance, the first impression given by the new service was of a teaching by withdrawal service, although this was not really the intention behind it. Since teachers liked, or were relatively happy with, withdrawal, the additional role of advice and in-class support was difficult for class teachers to grasp or accept. There was also considerable dismay among teachers about the developments in Midshire, where a number of new support systems were being set up, but little information about their intentions had reached class teachers. Making change acceptable to teachers seemed to be dependent on teachers' feelings of involvement and/or the LEAs' responsiveness to teacher requests.

The description of the children's days showed how differently similar types of support can be delivered to children. For example, one child who was withdrawn for special help did not get any follow-up in class of the work he did at his withdrawal session, because his class teacher did not know what this was. A second child who was withdrawn had the same practice work both in class and in withdrawal sessions; his class teacher was therefore aware of, and involved in, his (special) work although it was set by someone else. Similarly, the teacher of one child on an individual teaching programme had organized the class so that it did not take up too much time to check the child's progress on the teaching programme, while other teachers found this very difficult to manage and indeed one child observed on an individual programme was taken alone by the class teacher while the rest of the class went off to do something else.

Having said this, there were considerable similarities among all the children observed in the percentage of time spent in various activities and groupings. This suggests that our classrooms were 'typical' primary class-rooms whose overall organization and activities were similar to those found in the ORACLE research (Galton *et al*, 1980), and that children with special needs take up a good deal of teachers' time (as Croll and Moses (1985) also found) *whatever the system of support provided.* This helps to explain why an LEA that says it will provide advice to teachers but no (more) withdrawal teaching can almost be guaranteed a poor initial response from teachers. Children with special needs already take up much of their teachers' time.

Issues

We now turn to the issues raised in the Introduction.

Usefulness of Screening Programmes

As the results of our LEA survey showed(in chapter 2), screening is used to identify children who need extra help or support now, rather than as a predictive measure. Most of the LEAs that replied had screening pro-grammes. However, the LEA screening test may have very little impact on the way that teachers identify children who need help. Even in screening LEAs, teachers were unlikely to rely on the LEA screening test alone as a measure of identification. Indeed teachers rarely mentioned the screening programmes: the one thing the screening programmes had in common was a low profile in schools. Of course it would be surprising if experienced teachers had to wait for a child to be tested at 7+, for example, before knowing that he or she needed extra help. But not all teachers are experienced and not every child is noticed. The major role of screening programmes would, therefore, seem to be as a safety net, (a role which we have commented on before: Gipps *et al*, 1983). It can also be a way of estimating demand for a support service, though there is of course no guarantee that having identified a certain level of need, LEAs will be able to meet it directly from their resources. Indeed part of the rationale behind the new developments in support services was to get better value for money by having the class teacher as the client rather than individual children. In such a climate a centralized screening programme seems contradictory.

Screening programmes which involve checklists have a slightly different role: LEAs reported they had introduced checklists to sensitise teachers to children's development. Where schools had developed checklists for use at infant level, teachers indeed reported greater awareness of children's difficulties. This may also be the case where teachers administer a screening checklist rather than a test. This kind of screening, therefore, is different from screening using a standardized reading test, particularly where class teachers may have been involved in the development of the checklist.

Impact of Changes in Support Services: Teachers and Children

The impact of support service change is easier to assess for teachers than it is for children. By and large, in our case study LEAs, the impact of change has been to create more work for class teachers.

For the class teachers a change in support service could have either a positive or negative impact depending on whether the teachers felt they were experiencing a net gain or loss. At schools where there was previously very little help available a new service with a brief to visit every primary school was likely to be enthusiastically received even if, ironically, this meant more work on their part than before. Where schools had lost a part-timer who withdrew children for help, and had been given a twice termly visit by a new area coordinator, the response was likely to have been less positive.

Where children receive special help outside the classroom (as the majority still do) they may well have two separate experiences of education. There is little doubt which of the two experiences we described constitutes the more useful educational one: small group teaching with high levels of teacher-child interaction and discussion, sustained periods of quiet concentration, and tasks properly matched to the child's level of development. (Needless to say, this was not always what we observed in withdrawal sessions.) This dual experience is likely to continue until specialist teaching becomes integrated with classroom experience or teachers can, and do, cater for all children with special needs within their classes.

Where individual teaching programmes have been introduced, an issue is the time required to carry out these individual programmes of work, either to effect and superintend those developed elsewhere or to put together new ones. In some LEAs where these have been introduced, support staff have suggested restricting the number of children on programmes so that teachers can cope, certainly in the early stages of these new developments.

Classroom management, always an issue for primary teachers (HMI, 1978; Bennett *et al*, 1984), becomes even more important when such individual programmes are introduced. Given that we know teaching is just as likely to be aimed at classes or groups as at individuals (Barker Lunn, 1984) this is not surprising: primary teachers are not as used to teaching children individually as we might have expected.

Changes affect not only the class teacher but support service teachers as well. In cases where staff have been retained in a service that has changed its role, they will have more difficulty in promoting this new role than where new staff have been taken on. If previously a remedial teacher withdrew children but now intends to work alongside and offer advice to the class teacher, both class and support teachers may find it difficult to reconcile this with the previous situation. In Norborough, the new service itself has a similar problem, in that the staff started out by teaching and are only now gradually changing their role.

If an LEA takes a different route and reduces or removes its PRTs, by absorbing them into ordinary school-based posts (as Ruralshire did) or by not renewing their contracts (as Ruralshire planned to do originally) in order to hire new, differently qualified, support staff this is likely to cause upset, not only to the PRTs themselves, but in the schools where they have worked. Such a development, if it is seen as being handled badly by the LEA, (and this was not the case in *all* parts of Ruralshire) can of course jeopardize the success of the new service.

Staffing new support services can also be difficult if an LEA has to draw staff only from within its area. In Midshire new posts were advertised locally rather than nationally since this was LEA policy, and there was a feeling in schools that some members of the support staff were not sufficiently well qualified or trained. However it is likely that this was in part due to the large number of new staff taken on within a short space of time. In Norborough, where similarly all new staff were local teachers, this was not the case, but the new staff had been taken on in smaller numbers.

One way of increasing the pool of special needs expertise is to second staff into posts in the support service and allow them to return to schools after two or three years, and two of our case study LEAs were doing this. However, the idea was not popular with the staff concerned: once out of a class teaching job, they did not wish to go back to it. They aimed to stay in the support service, or go on to a deputy headship. The intention behind secondments of this kind may therefore be counter-productive, actually reducing the numbers of interested teachers in schools, rather than increasing them.

Management of Change

The five case study LEAs in which major developments were happening had all adopted different ways of introducing and managing the new developments. We believe that much can be learned from the management of change in Newtown. There the support team was reduced from ten to four and the responsibility for children with special needs was thrust firmly on to the class teacher. These two factors, one might expect, would lead to dissatisfied class teachers but, on the contrary, the teachers in Newtown were the most satisfied group in our study.

The initial presentation of developments in Newtown was a letter to all primary heads from the Chief Inspector explaining the LEA's plan for special needs provision in ordinary schools. The letter asked heads to select a term over the next six when a member of staff could go on a six-session learning difficulties course. This followed work by a development team on materials, as well as a pilot course involving a range of primary schools in the LEA. All the heads were themselves invited to a one-day session where they were introduced to the philosophy behind the developments. Heads were given a handbook, which described the special needs programme, contained suggested checklists for identification and gave details of the support agencies within the LEA. These were meant for display in all staffrooms. Heads at this session were also asked to choose the school's representative (special needs coordinator, SNC) carefully, bearing in mind the importance of their future role as communicators of the programme back to the school.

The intention from the start was to make the whole activity very high profile, and the method of presentation was completely straight: schools knew from the word go what it would mean for them. Teachers' suggestions and modifications were incorporated into the course with development continuing throughout. In-service training already had a high commitment from the LEA (£100,000 a year in 1985/6) and was very much a way of life for teachers in Newtown, which made the LEA's task easier. The four support team members, who now had an advisory role, went into schools *after* the course and thus provided support, either materials or information, at the crucial stage of transfer of information within school; this must have made the SNCs' role easier.

Demands from some despairing teachers for help in the classroom with the teaching materials and approach, resulted in some of the support team working with children on a short term basis, rather than restricting their role to advising as originally intended, and 'spare' teachers helping with this too.

This is in contrast to the approach in another case study LEA when it was decided to remove part-time remedial posts from schools. The heads received a letter telling them that since the allocation panel was swamped with requests for help for the '18 per cent child' the school-based remedial posts would go in order to strengthen the support services. The fact was that these part-time posts were a historical anomaly: the children for whom they were originally allocated had moved on to secondary school. It was, therefore, high time to reconsider this allocation and the LEA decided to centralize resources. This part of the explanation was not in the letter to heads and might well have helped them to understand the move. As it was presented it did little to win the teachers over to the LEA's cause. Having said that, we have yet to come across a school that did not mind losing its 0.4 or 0.5 teacher. The significance of this small resource is enormous for the schools, and LEAs which remove them do so at their peril!

The Impact of the 1981 Act and Cuts in Expenditure

The impact of the cuts in educational expenditure on the support services was much less than we had anticipated when we planned the study. On the contrary, the picture was one of holding expenditure steady, if not of modest expansion. This is due in part to the gradual snowballing of developments in special needs, and no doubt Education Committee members' realization that they have responsibilities to a wider group than the small percentage who require a statement of special needs. Our analysis is that without the lever of the 1981 Act, support services would have been cut more than they have and the move to change — which was being urged by the remedial profession in the late 1970s — would not have maintained its impetus.[1]

Thus the 1981 Act has enabled special needs provision in LEAs to develop in spite of the cuts, rather than for the cuts to have acted as a brake on developments.

Models of Support

We now look at the pros and cons of the two main models of support: withdrawal teaching and individual support in class from the class teacher. The latter includes situations in which the class teacher is supported by advice, materials, in-service training and/or individual teaching programmes. We stress the dichotomy between withdrawal and 'the rest', because it became clear to us that as far as the children are concerned this is the major distinction.

Withdrawal

We have already referred to two types of educational experience for some of the children we observed. Where withdrawal is used just for hearing the children read, then the experience is not a useful educational one. It could be seen as having more of a socio-emotional role: pleasurable 'time-out' for the child, an occasional reduction in class numbers for the teacher and the feeling that 'something' is being done for that child. But there are other advantages. Teachers referred to children's increased confidence and we observed children in completely different persona in the different settings, which suggested that personal-social development was likely to be a benefit. The different relationship between child and class teacher and child and remedial teacher must also be considered. One of the strengths of the British primary school is the class teacher system, but as Thomas (ILEA, 1985) points out, there are bound to be casualties. Some teachers do not get on with some children; some teachers do not find it easy to help or teach some children. The opportunity for children to spend time with another adult with whom they can communicate, feel relaxed, or whatever, must be to their advantage. *We never saw a child unwilling to go to a withdrawal session*, in fact rather the reverse. We rarely saw a child bored and switched-off in a short withdrawal session (although we did in a long, half-day withdrawal session in a remedial centre). The exception was a child in a withdrawal session with her class teacher. We feel that these points mark important benefits for the child and should not be ignored because withdrawal is no longer fashionable.

We did observe some withdrawal that *was* educationally positive: good 'match', high concentration, time on task, good liaison, and so on. We are not advocating withdrawal as the best single method of helping children with special needs but we are struck by the fact that 'good' withdrawal has much to offer and that class teachers have good reason to see it as being of help.

By 'good' withdrawal we mean regular sessions (at a fixed time which the child can rely on and arranged so that it does not deprive him of something potentially more enjoyable or unusual) in a small group, with a well-trained specialist remedial/support teacher, on a carefully planned work programme, which is matched to the child's capabilities and related to the child's class work, so that practice or routine work is common between class and withdrawal session. In 'good' withdrawal the class teacher specifically does *not* abandon her responsibilities for the child to someone else. This of course suggests — indeed demands — full, regular liaison between class teacher and support teacher.

This is not impossible. It is how the best BSST teachers in Norborough worked at the time of our visits. Where it worked well, it worked extremely well, and it would be interesting to see whether the aim of the LEA is still to move to a full advisory model. That said it does demand high levels of support staffing which may only be possible in (small) metropolitan authorities which have access to extra resources from the Inner Area scheme.

The other side of the coin is 'bad' withdrawal. By this we mean the hearing-them-read syndrome which we have already described at the start of this section. That parents are being used to fulfil this role in many schools indicates that it is not necessarily an 'educational' activity which requires a highly qualified professional teacher. Negative aspects of withdrawal also include irregular timing/sessions and lack of liaison between class teacher and special teacher. Where there is no liaison at all to speak of (and where the withdrawal is physically distant) for the child it is equivalent to going to the dentist in terms of the extent to which the activity impinges on his classroom experience.

Support from the Class Teacher

Given that support services in many LEAs cannot be of the size needed to work via the child directly, but must instead work through the class teacher, we now consider some of these approaches.

a)   Individual teaching programmes

Individual teaching programmes can be of various kinds. They can range from a collection of ready made materials selected after diagnostic assessment by the teacher (as in Suburb), or by the support service (as in Norborough), to teacher-made teaching objectives type programmes (as in Newtown).

The use of behavioural objectives to plan curricula for teaching developed in this country in the early 1970s in schools for the mentally handicapped (Swann, 1983). By the late 1970s it was being taken up in ESN(M) schools. A number of educational psychologists have advocated this approach for children with difficulties in learning basic skills in ordinary schools to teach some aspects of literacy and maths. This is considered to be necessary for some children who do not learn 'incidentally' or 'spontaneously' but who require highly structured and planned learning experiences. This view is in fact criticized by Swann (*ibid*) on the grounds that concentrating on the teaching approach tends to limit consideration of the content of teaching which, he argues, must be relevant to the experience of the children concerned. He also rejects the notion that some children will only learn if the teaching material is carefully structured according to objectives, and argues that this approach makes it likely that these children's experience will be strongly directed towards basic skills which in effect segregates them in the classroom. Other psychologists see the lack of prescribed content as a strength; only the approach is specified, so the content may be left up to the class teacher and thus it should be more acceptable to teachers (for example, Leach, 1980). There are, however, teachers who see the teaching objectives approach as being at odds with their vision of primary education and the emphasis on 'tight' structure as threatening to discovery and creativity in the classroom. It is at odds with the process approach to the curriculum which is expounded by many supporters of progressive primary education (Blenkin and Kelly, 1981) but it does have in common with it the emphasis on individualized curricula. There is a certain amount of mystique attached to the teaching objectives approach and indeed much of what is practised in primary schools under this label is a much watered-down version of what was used with mentally handicapped children. Basically, the teacher identifies clearly the learning outcome which is desired and indicates the progression, or small learning steps, which are required for the child to achieve this objective.

Whatever the arguments for or against teaching objectives, we have described teachers (in Suburb and Newtown) working more or less happily with individual teaching programmes. However, they operated with very different levels of efficiency in terms of classroom management. Since classroom management is obviously crucial in the delivery of this sort of approach it cannot be left to chance, or trial and error, but must be included as part of the in-service training to support the individual programmes.

Ironically, it is the very individualization of the programmes which causes most practical difficulties for class teachers, the time needed to get round to children on individual programmes being a particular problem. However, concern about the concentration on basic skills within the programmes did not seem to be an issue. A bonus of the approach was that teachers felt children were able to see that they were making progress; for many of them this was a welcome change.

This bonus was reported by teachers in Newtown and in Suburb, particularly on the newer reading packs in Suburb. The two systems worked rather differently, however, and children in Suburb tended to work less well than some of those observed in Newtown. This may have been to do with the difference in the types of programmes. In Newtown, the teacher (or SNC) draws up a short programme with the goal to be achieved and the steps necessary to achieve that goal, and the child works through those steps. Because, ideally, the teacher designs the steps and the goals, they can be changed if difficulties arise. In Suburb, flexibility is represented by the range of available worksheets or packs. These may not be related directly to the child's curriculum. A child may therefore be practising a particular skill, for example sound blending, on a series of worksheets. Assessment of progress is either measured through successful completion of the sheets or, in the case of the newer packs, by the daily checking of a child's performance of a particular task. The newer aspect is similar to Newtown, but the traditional practice worksheets are reminiscent of the practice work described in Norborough. In Suburb, it was not uncommon to see children wading, bored, through a series of repetitive sheets.

The children's interest and ability to do the work without constant supervision must reflect the nature and content of the programmes them-selves and suggests that individual programmes are better if designed specifically for a child to suit their curriculum.

b) *In-service training*

The other method of supporting the child via the class teacher is by giving in-service training to class teachers. The feeling we got from Midshire and Ruralshire was that in-service training alone was not enough. It needs to be accompanied by the provision of material (Norborough) and/or a specific approach (Newtown). It is clear from the questionnaire that many teachers did not regard in-service as a form of support and, as we know from research in this area, as a general rule in-service training on the centre-periphery model is not particularly effective. However, the DES's One-Term In-Service (OTIS) programme which provides one-term full-time courses for school SNC/link teachers should have more effect, and the aim is to have one of these trained teachers in every primary school. (This, however, will take at least ten to fifteen years.) Each primary school would then have a special needs specialist on the staff in the way that the DES has suggested there should be subject specialists (DES, 1985).

A point which we should like to make about 'good' withdrawal is that it can be seen as a form of in-service training. Since the liaison between class teacher and support teacher should involve detailed discussion of teaching method and content, the class teacher can gain expertise which is used to help other children. The process thus becomes one of in-service training, albeit slow, in which the class teacher is enabled to develop her own skills whilst at the same time getting some specialist help.

To conclude this section, in-service training particularly of the kind carried out part-time after school is not enough. It is, however, a vital part of new developments whether for passing on information to teachers and schools, or for supporting the introduction of a new teaching approach or programme. Individual teaching programmes seem to be more acceptable to teachers if they are introduced as part of a major LEA development; they seem to work better if designed by class teachers; however introduced they demand careful classroom management. The HMI primary survey (DES, 1978b) suggested that teachers should move around more and stop having queues at their tables; this is just as important for teachers coping with children with special needs.

So what is the best deal for the child? We know from other research that the answer is a system that maximizes concentration, interest, time on task, and higher order cognitive interactions between adult and child. Similarly it should be one that minimizes distraction, work at an inappropriate level, and 'special' work unrelated to classroom work.

We think this chapter has shown that there are a number of routes to a best deal. It can be done by involving teachers in developing assessment and teaching materials (as in Suburb), by massive in-service training programmes and the acceptance of a particular teaching approach (as in Newtown), or by regular on-the-hoof input from the support teacher to the class teacher in 'good' withdrawal (as in Norborough). Each of these developments has worked well in its own place.

What we are saying is that there is no one 'best' model for helping children with special needs in primary schools, *as long as class teachers are involved*. What is crucial is that the teachers feel engaged with it. You can persuade teachers to take on any model, within reason, if only you set about it the right way: communicate clearly, openly and regularly, offer good support for the model, be responsive to teacher concern and complaint, involve the teachers in the development.

There are those who would argue that dissatisfaction, such as that shown in Midshire, is an essential part of change. We do not agree. Some level of uncertainty and concern may be inevitable, but dissatisfaction is not inevitable. There is no research evidence to show that there is a link between teacher satisfaction and children's progress, but given that primary education is about far more than learning to read we believe that it is ill-advised for LEAs not to try to carry the teachers with them in new developments.

There is another model of improving children's reading skills which we mentioned in chapter 1 and this is parental help with reading. Since the initial Haringey study in the late 1970s, the practice has mushroomed all over the country; we might consider it to be the biggest growth area in reading. If parental involvement with reading can improve children's reading performance, then of course it will reduce the number of children with special needs in this area, and this is to be welcomed.

Messages

Finally, the findings of this project and our discussion of them have produced a number of messages for LEAs and schools.

(i)   Given the low level of usage of screening test results at classroom level, some LEAs will no doubt wish to reconsider whether screening is worthwhile, particularly if the emphasis is on help coming from the class teacher's own resources rather than from an external support service. In that situation, school-based checklists and careful record keeping would be of more use to the teacher and child. The LEA, of course, may wish to collect test scores for other, managerial, purposes but then the programme should not, strictly speaking, be called a screening programme.

(ii)   An area that created difficulty, particularly where advice and materials were on offer, was time for liaison. If teachers are having to do more because of the increased emphasis on their role in special needs and there is, at the same time, less part-time staffing in school, class teachers may have little time for liaison with visiting support staff. Liaison between remedial/support teacher and class teacher is not difficult, but it does require systematic attention. If left to chance it is too easily forgotten. For this reason arrangements where support staff are in a school for half a day or more are much more satisfactory than shorter visits: in the days before the 1985/86 teachers' dispute liaison could take place at dinnertime or the morning break. In the aftermath of that dispute liaison at those times may be in jeopardy. Whenever it takes place, however, such liaison must entail more than the routine 'How is Shane getting on?' niceties, and focus on the actual content of that child's curriculum and the pedagogical approaches used. The other advantage of support staff being in school for half a day rather than shorter spells is that they have a better chance of getting to know the staff and becoming part of the school. This in turn will make it more likely that other staff will ask them for support and advice.

(iii) Communication about changes or developments needs to be clear, open and responsive. Defensiveness is not persuasive and will probably be counter-productive. Mismatch between LEA and school can easily occur and as chapters 6 and 7 showed often causes problems.

(iv) There is also a message here about LEAs buying-in packages which have been developed in other LEAs. Such developments have usually involved tremendous staff input, involvement and commitment. These factors are crucial to the success of the development in the home LEA; they are generally missing when the package is bought by another LEA and the outcome in new LEAs is often disappointing. This is what happened with the Croydon Checklist, which was developed originally as part of an in-service exercise, but exported as a simple checklist on two sides of A4 paper. Similarly, the reading programme developed in Barking, when evaluated in the early stages, had raised the reading ages of a sample of children in the LEA by an average of twenty months in an eight-month period. The involvement of local teachers in the development of this programme and materials seems to have been crucial, for when they were exported to a neighbouring London borough and 'imposed' on teachers there, (because time available for in-service support was limited) results were very disappointing (Trickey and Kosky, 1983). We became aware during our visits to the six case study LEAs, and elsewhere, that the same thing is in danger of happening, unfortunately, with Coventry's SNAP programme. This package again involved a massive development programme in its originating LEA. What is being bought by other LEAs however is an approach, checklists and other materials — but not the in-service training, the commitment, dedication, back-up and charismatic support of the originators.

The message to LEAs then is this: buy a package or checklist from another LEA by all means, but do not expect it to be a miracle cure in your LEA. Using it as part of your own in-service programme and involving your teachers in modifying it to suit local needs will help your staff to feel that it is 'theirs', which may well increase its effectiveness.

(v) Finally, all the models would benefit from smaller classes, but reducing class size alone is not the answer. This leads us to the major message for teachers which is that improving the education of children with special needs is not going to be easy. It will involve more work — whether in training, preparation of materials, liaison with specialist staff, contact with the child, or all of these. However it is unrealistic to expect class teachers to make these changes and improvements without adequate support from the LEA.

To conclude, the picture is a positive one of development and change in special needs provision. Unfortunately, much of this has happened in the absence of clear information about the best way to improve support for these children or about the implications for classrooms of some of the developments. Our aim has been that this study should contribute something to the picture. What we have concluded is that there is no one 'best deal' for supporting children with special needs in primary school. There are a number of options which LEAs can take to improve support to these children and the choice depends on the LEA size, resources available and previous arrangements. Also, that teachers can make any system work well, or badly. What has come through to us most strongly in this study, and we hope we have communicated, is that where children were getting a good deal it was where services had been developed in a spirit of cooperation between teachers and the LEA. Such a partnership must be possible even in geographically large LEAs. The vast majority of the teachers we spoke to were genuinely concerned to help these children and it was a shame to see this goodwill dissipated occasionally by bad management. LEAs want to make the changes work too, and such a partnership is the least that we can ask of those whose responsibility it is to support children with special needs in primary schools.

Note

1   We should point out that the bulk of our school visits took place before the peak of the teachers' industrial action in 1985/86 and the goodwill required on the part of class teachers to make these changes was still largely available.

References

AINSCOW, M. and MUNCEY, J. (1983) 'Learning difficulties in the primary school: An in-service training initiative', *Remedial Education*, 18, 3.

AINSCOW, M. and TWEDDLE D.A. (1979) *Preventing Classroom Failure*, John Wiley.

BARKER LUNN, J. (1984) 'Junior school teachers: Their methods and practices', *Educational Research*, 26, 3.

BARTON, L. and TOMLINSON, S. (1981) *Special Education: Policy, Practices and Social Issues*, London, Harper and Row.

~ETT, N., DESFORGES, C., COCKBURN, A. and WILKINSON, B. (1984) *The Quality of Pupil Learning Experiences*, London, Lawrence Erlbaum Associates Ltd.

BERGER, M., YULE, W. and RUTTER, M. (1975) 'Attainment and adjustment in two geographical areas: II The prevalence of specific reading retardation', *British Journal of Psychiatry*, 126, pp. 510–19.

BLENKIN, G. and KELLY, A.V. (1981) *The Primary Curriculum*, London, Harper and Row.

BRYANT, P. and BRADLEY, L. (1985) *Children's Reading Problems*, Oxford, Blackwell.

BURT, C. (1921) *Mental and Scholastic Tests*, London, P.S. KING and Son.

CAMERON, R.J. (1982) 'Teaching and evaluating curriculum objectives', *Remedial Education*, 17, 3.

CARROLL, H.C.M. (1972) 'The remedial teaching of reading: An Evaluation', *Remedial Education*, 7, 1.

CASHDAN, A., PUMPHREY, P. and LUNZER, E.A. (1971) 'Children receiving remedial teaching in reading', *Educational Research*, 13, 2.

CLARK, M.M. (1979) 'Why remedial?' in GAINS, C.W. and McNICHOLAS, J.A. (Eds.) *Remedial Education: Guidelines for the Future*, London, Longman.

CLIFT, P. (1970) *Factors affecting the Growth of Reading Skills in Children aged 8–9 who are Backward in Reading*, unpublished MEd thesis, University of Manchester.

COLLINS, J.E. (1961) *The Effects of Remedial Education*, London, Oliver and Boyd.

CORNWALL, K. (1979) 'The Development of a Screening Technique: Some Reflections on Four Years Experience in One LEA', Occasional Papers of the Division of Educational and Child Psychology, 3, 1.

CORNWALL, K., HEDDERLY, R. and PUMPHREY, P. (1983) 'Specific Learning Difficulties: the 'Specific Reading Difficulties' Versus 'Dyslexia' Controversy Resolved?', Occasional Papers of the Division of Education and Child Psychology, 7, 3.

CORNWALL, K. and SPICER, J. (1983) 'The Role of the Educational Psychologist in the Discovery and Assessment of Children Requiring Special Education', *Occasional Papers of the Division of Education and Child Psychology*.

CROLL, P. and MOSES, D. (1985) *One in Five*, London, Routledge and Kegan Paul.

CURTIS, A. and WIGNALL, M. (1981) *Early Learning: Assessment and Development*, MacMillan Education.

DAVIE, R., BUTLER, N. and GOLDSTEIN, H. (1972) *From Birth to Seven*, London, Longman/National Children's Bureau.

DEPARTMENT of EDUCATION and SCIENCE (1972) *Children with Specific Reading Difficulties*, London, HMSO.

DEPARTMENT of EDUCATION and SCIENCE (1975) *A Language for Life* (The Bullock Report), London, HMSO.

DEPARTMENT of EDUCATION and SCIENCE (1978a) *Special Educational Needs* (The Warnock Report), London, HMSO.

DEPARTMENT of EDUCATION and SCIENCE (1978b) *Primary Education in England: A Survey by HM Inspectors of Schools*, London, HMSO.

DEPARTMENT of EDUCATION and SCIENCE (1981) *Education Act*, London, HMSO.

DEPARTMENT of EDUCATION and SCIENCE (1983) *Report by Her Majesty's Inspectors on the Effects of Local Authority Expenditure Policies on the Education Service in England — 1982*, London, HMSO.

DEPARTMENT of EDUCATION and SCIENCE (1985) *Better Schools*, London, HMSO.

EVANS, R., DAVIES, P., FERGUSON, N. and WILLIAMS, P. (1979) *Swansea Evaluation Profiles for School Entrants*, Windsor, NFER/Nelson.

FOGELMAN, K. (Ed.) (1976) *Britain's 16 Year Olds*, London, National Children's Bureau.

GAINS, C.W. (1980) 'Remedial education in the 1980s', *Remedial Education*, 15, 1.

GAINS, C.W. and McNICHOLAS, J.A. (Eds.) (1979) *Remedial Education: Guidelines for the Future*, London, Longman.

GALTON, M., SIMON, B. and CROLL, P. (1980) *Inside the Primary Classroom*, London, Routledge and Kegan Paul.

GIPPS, C., GOLDSTEIN, H. and GROSS, H. (1985) 'Twenty per cent with special educational needs: Another legacy from Cyril Burt?', *Remedial Education*, 20, 2.

GIPPS, C., STEADMAN, S.D., BLACKSTONE, T. and STIERER, B. (1983) *Testing Children: Standardised Testing in Local Education Authorities and Schools*, London, Heinemann Educational Books.

GITTELMAN, R. and FEINGOLD, I. (1983) 'Children with reading disorders — Efficacy of reading remediation', *Journal of Child Psychology and Psychiatry*, 24, 2.

GOLBY, M. and GULLIVER, J. (1979) 'Whose remedies, whose ills? A critical review of remedial education', *Journal of Curriculum Studies*, 11, 2, pp. 137–47.

GROSS, H. and GIPPS, C. (1987) *Supporting Warnock's Eighteen Per Cent: Six Case Studies*, Lewes, Falmer Press.

HALE, A. (1980) 'The social relationships implicit in approaches to reading', *Reading* 14, 2.

HELLER, K., HOLTZMAN, W. and MESSICK, S. (1982) *Placing Children in Special Education: A Strategy for Equity*, Washington DC, National Academy Press.

ILEA (1985) *Improving Primary Schools* (The Thomas Report), London, ILEA.

ILEC (1974) Minutes of the ILE Committee quoted in the Warnock Report (DES, 1978), p. 40.

JACKSON, A. and HANNON, P. (1981) *The Belfield Reading Project*, Rochdale, Belfield

Community Council.

KEOGH, B. and BECKER, L. (1973) 'Early detection of learning problems: Questions, cautions and guidelines', *Exceptional Children*, 40, pp. 5–11.

KINGSLAKE, B. (1983) 'The predictive (in) accuracy of on-entry to school screening procedures when used to anticipate learning difficulties', *Special Education: Forward Trends*, 10, 4.

LEACH, D. (1980) 'Assessing children with learning difficulties: An alternative model for psychologists and teachers', *Association of Educational Psychologists Journal*, 5, 3.

LEACH, D. (1981) 'Early screening for school learning difficulties: Efficacy, problems and alternatives', Occasional Papers of Division of Educational and Child Psychology, 5, 2.

LINDSAY, G.A. (1979) 'The Early Identification of Learning Difficulties and the monitoring of Children's Progress', unpublished PhD thesis, Birmingham.

LINDSAY, G.A. (1980) 'The infant rating scale', *British Journal of Educational Psychology*, 50, 2.

LINDSAY, G.A. (1984) *Screening for Children with Special Needs*, London, Croom Helm Ltd.

LINDSAY, G.A. and PEARSON, L. (1981) *Identification and Intervention School Based Approaches*, TRC Publishing Ltd.

LINDSAY, G.A. and WEDELL, K. (1982) 'The early identification of educationally "At Risk" children revisited', *Journal of Learning Difficulties*, 15, 4.

LOVELL, K., JOHNSON, E. and PLATTS, D. (1962) 'A summary of a study of the reading ages of children who had been given remedial teaching', *British Journal of Educational Psychology*, 32.

MABEY, C. (1982) quoted in GOODACRE, E. 'Reading research in Great Britain — 1981', *Reading*, 16, 2.

MEEK, M. *et al.*, (1983) *Achieving Literacy*, London, Methuen.

MOSELEY, D. (1969) 'The talking typewriter and remedial teaching in a secondary school', *Remedial Education*, 4, pp. 196–202.

MOSELEY, D. (1975) *Special Provision for Reading*, Slough, NFER.

MOSES, D. (1982) 'Special educational needs: The relationship between teacher assessment, test scores and classroom behaviour', *British Educational Research Journal*, 8, 2.

MOYLE, D. (1982) 'Recent developments in reading and their effects upon remedial education', *Remedial Education*, 17, 4.

NUT, (1982) *Schools Speak Out: The Effects of Expenditure Cuts on Primary Education*, London, NUT.

POTTON, A. (1983) *Screening*, London, MacMillan.

POTTS, P. (1982) *Biology and Handicap*, Unit 11 of E241 Special Needs in Education, Milton Keynes, Open University Press.

PRINGLE, M.L.K., BUTLER, N. and DAVIE, R. (1966) *11,000 Seven Year Olds*, London, Longman.

PROSSER, M. (1981) 'The Myth of parental apathy', *TES*, 16 October 1981, pp. 22–3.

RENNIE, E. (1980) 'The West Riding screening six years on', *Educational Research*, 23, 1.

RESCHLY, D.J. (1983) The Right Questions (Finally!): Comments on the NAS Report on Mild Mental Retardation Classification/Placement, paper given at annual meeting of AERA, Montreal, April.

Rutter, M., Cox, A., Tupling, C., Berger, M. and Yule, W. (1975) 'Attainment and adjustment in two geographical areas: I the prevalence of psychiatric disorder', *British Journal of Psychiatry*, 126, pp. 493–509.

Rutter, M., Tizard, J. and Whitmore, K. (Eds.) (1970) *Education, Health and Behaviour*, London, Longman.

Satz, P. and Fletcher, J. (1979) 'Early screening tests: some uses and abuses, *Journal of Learning Disability*, 12.

Schrag, P. and Divoky, D. (1975) *The Myth of the Hyperactive Child'*, New York, Dell Publishing.

Shepard, L.A. (1983) 'The role of measurement in educational policy: Lessons from the identification of learning disabilities', *Educational Measurement: Issues and Practice*, London, Routledge and Kegan Paul.

Shepard, L.A., Smith, M.L. and Vojir, C.P. (1983) 'Characteristics of pupils identified as learning disabled', *American Educational Research Journal*, 20, 3.

Spencer, M. (1980) 'Handing down the magic', in Salmon, P. (Ed.) *Coming to Know*.

Stierer, B. (1984) *Parental Help with Reading in Schools*, Project Report, University of London Institute of Education.

Sutton, A. (1981) 'The social role of educational psychology in the definition of educational subnormality', in Barton, L. and Tomlinson, S. (Eds.), *Special Education: Policy, Practices and Social Issues*, London, Harper and Row.

Swann, W. (1983) 'Curriculum principles for integration', in Booth, T. and Potts, P. (Eds.) *Integrating Special Education*, Oxford, Blackwell.

Tansley, A.E. (1967) *Reading and Remedial Reading*, London, Routlege and Kegan Paul.

Tansley, P. and Pankhurst, J. (1981) *Children with Specific Learning Difficulties: A Critical Review of Research*, Windsor, NFER.

TES (1985) 'Banding based on opinion of blacks' behaviour', 25 October.

Tizard, J., Schofield, W. and Hewison, J. (1982) 'Collaboration between teachers and parents in assisting children's reading', *British Journal of Educational Psychology*, 52, 1.

Topping, K. (1985) 'Review and prospect', in Topping, K. and Wolfendale, S. (Eds.) *Parental Involvement in Children's Reading*, London, Croom Helm.

Trickey, G. and Daly, B. (1977) 'Diagnosing readers', *TES*, 5 August.

Trickey, G. and Kosky, R. (1983) 'The Barking Project: Organizing for diversity', *Remedial Education*, 18, 2.

Webb, L. (1967) *Children with Special Needs in the Infants School*, Gerrards, Smythe (published in 1969 by Fontana).

Wedell, K. (1980) 'Early identification and compensatory interaction', in Knight, R. and Bakker, D. *Treatment of Hyperactive and Learning Disordered Children: Current Research*, Baltimore, University Press.

Wedell, K. (1981) 'Concepts of special educational need', *Education Today*, 31, pp. 3–9.

Wedell, K. and Lindsay, G. (1980) 'Early identification procedures: What have we learned?', *Remedial Education*, 15, 3.

Wolfendale, S. and Bryans, T. (1979) *Identification of Learning Difficulties: A Model for Intervention*, NARE.

Woods J. (1978) The provision of extra reading help in ILEA Secondary Schools,

References

ILEA Research and Statistics Branch RS 689/78.

YOUNG, P. and TYRE, C. (1983) *Dyslexia or Illiteracy? Realising the Right to Read*, Milton Keynes, Open University Press.

YULE, W. 1973, 'Differential diagnosis of reading backwardness and special educational retardation', *British Journal of Educational Psychology*, 43.

Index

Advice to class teacher 38, 39, 65, 68, 82, 122
Adviser/Inspector 24, 26, 36, 41–2
Adviser, remedial 29, 41
Adviser, special needs 29, 41, 62
Advisory Teacher 36, 43, 86, 121
Assessment 6, 10, 15, 16, 21, 22, 29, 30, 37, 38, 42, 44, 50 54, 60, 73, 84, 91, 129, 132
(see also Testing)

Barking Reading Project 6, 134
Basic skills 92, 96, 106, 109, 113, 115, 129–30
Behaviour problems 10, 39, 92, 111
Bullock Report 4, 16, 35, 36, 46

Carver Reading Test 54, 55, 101
Case study LEAs, description of 48–64
Checklist 16, 17, 20, 21, 24, 26–28, 31, 34, 60, 62, 120, 124, 126, 133 134
Children 91–119
Classroom management 11, 118, 125, 130, 132
Class size 3, 67, 69, 71–73, 77, 78, 80–1, 122, 134
Class teacher 38–40, 43, 44, 46, 50, 57, 59, 62, 64–91, 93, 95–97, 100, 101, 103, 105, 106, 108–117, 120–125, 128–133, 135
Concentration 96–99, 103, 109–110, 114, 116, 128, 132
Croydon checklist 134
County councils 39, 41, 56, 61, 75

Curriculum 2, 6–8, 11, 21, 22, 28, 59, 86, 87, 92, 111, 115, 117 129–131, 133
Cut-off score 12–14, 19, 20, 28–30, 34, 45, 120
Cuts in educational expenditure 1, 2–4, 28, 35, 42, 43, 46, 56, 59, 64, 65, 73–75, 121, 127

Department of Education & Science 16, 131
Dyslexia 8, 11, 47, 51, 63, 78

Education Act, 1981 9, 11, 14, 35, 37, 38, 40, 42, 43, 45, 46, 64, 65, 127
Educational psychologist 11, 16, 18, 20, 24, 26, 28–30, 36, 41–44, 46, 108, 121, 129–30
Evaluation of provision 44
Evaluation of screening 17, 18, 20, 30, 31, 34, 120

Falling rolls 3, 42, 45
Fidgetting 92, 96, 103, 106, 107, 115
Follow up 15, 28, 30, 56, 122

Head Teacher 3, 26, 30, 76, 85, 115, 126–7
HMI 2, 3
HMI Primary Survey 118, 132

Identification (includes early identification) 7, 10, 15–23, 24–34,

48, 60, 120, 123, 126
Inner area funding 48, 129
In-service training 6, 28, 34, 38, 39, 45, 58–63, 67, 69–72, 85, 87, 89, 115, 120, 121, 126, 130–134
Integration 7, 15
Intervention 18, 20, 21, 39
Isle of Wight survey 6, 12

Liaison 64, 71, 81, 83, 86, 95, 114, 116, 128, 129, 131, 133, 135
Literacy 7, 8, 44, 92
London Boroughs 39, 41, 42, 134

Management of Change 126–127
Maths 44, 92
Maths Tests 26
Metropolitan authorities 39, 41, 42, 48, 88
Mismatch 85–87, 122, 134
Mixed age classes 3, 67

National Association for Remedial Education 6

Parental Involvement in Reading 4, 8, 9
Parents 4, 53, 81, 98, 108, 129, 132
Part time teacher/staff 35, 36, 46, 56, 71, 74, 75, 89–80, 84, 101, 108, 111, 121, 122, 124, 127, 133
Pedagogy 22, 133
Peripatetic Remedial Teacher (PRT) 35, 36, 39, 41–43, 52, 57, 58, 64, 69, 71, 75, 76, 89, 105, 107, 125
Phonics 5, 8, 94, 98, 100, 101, 103, 109
Prediction (& paradox of) 16–18, 20, 21, 31, 121, 123
Pupil Teacher Radio 69
(see also class size)

Reading Age 10, 45, 52, 134
Reading Tests 4–6, 26, 29, 31, 33, 120
Records/Record keeping 28, 30–34, 44, 101, 104, 111, 112, 121, 133
Remedial Advisory Teacher (RAT) 28, 41–43, 57, 69, 71
Remedial centre 5, 35, 36, 51–53, 64, 71, 73, 98–100, 117

Remedial, definition of 2
Remedial service 2–4, 30, 36, 40, 41
(see also support service)
Remedial/SN support staff 3, 13, 17, 26, 29, 30, 37, 39, 41–46, 73–75, 82
(see also PRT, RAT)
Remedial teaching 1, 2
Remedial teaching, changes in 6–8
Remedial teaching, effectiveness of 4–6, 13
Resources 18, 27, 29, 33, 35, 37, 45, 71, 79, 83, 87, 111, 124, 133

Schools Psychological Service (SPS) 21, 28, 30, 36, 54, 55, 63, 73–88, 101, 111
Screening 14, 15–23, 24–34, 54, 56, 67, 94, 98, 120, 121, 123, 124, 133
Section II funding 48, 108
Slow learning children 53, 63, 71, 73, 92, 106
Special Needs Action Programme (SNAP) 22, 115, 134
Special Needs Coordinator (SNC) 59, 78, 86, 107, 126, 131
Special Needs, definition of 1, 2, 9–11
Special Needs, numbers of children 11–13, 19, 122
Special Needs, provision for 35–47
Special schools 19, 48
Specific learning difficulties 51
Specific reading difficulties (see dyslexia)
Statement (of SEN) 37, 127
Support service 28, 30, 36–38, 48, 77, 81, 83–85, 121, 127, 133
(see also remedial service)

Teacher training/qualifications 66, 67
Teaching materials 38, 39, 50, 54–56, 68–82, 84, 88, 126, 130
Teaching objectives 15, 21, 22, 28, 50, 57, 61, 85, 129, 130
(see also below)
Teaching programmes (including individual teaching programmes) 43, 50, 68, 85, 86, 88, 108, 110, 111, 116–118, 121–125, 129–131, 132

Testing 15, 25–34, 121
 (see also assessment)

Warnock Report 1, 2, 6, 8, 9, 11–13,
 17, 30, 35–6, 41, 45, 46, 120, 121
Withdrawal Teaching 6, 7, 35–38, 40,
 43, 50, 65, 68, 70, 84, 86, 91, 95, 96,
100, 103–107, 110, 114, 116, 117,
 118, 121–124, 128–9, 131–2
Worksheets/cards 55, 102, 105–6, 108,
 112, 131

Young's Group Reading Test 26,
 104

The Middle East

Other books in the Current Controversies series:

The Abortion Controversy
Alcoholism
Assisted Suicide
Biodiversity
Capital Punishment
Censorship
Child Abuse
Civil Liberties
Computers and Society
Conserving the Environment
Crime
Developing Nations
The Disabled
Drug Abuse
Drug Legalization
Drug Trafficking
Espionage and Intelligence
    Gathering
Ethics
Europe
Family Violence
Free Speech
Garbage and Waste
Gay Rights
Genetic Engineering
Guns and Violence
Hate Crimes
Homosexuality
Hunger
Illegal Drugs
Illegal Immigration

The Information Age
Interventionism
Iraq
Issues in Adoption
Marriage and Divorce
Medical Ethics
Mental Health
Minorities
Nationalism and Ethnic
    Conflict
Native American Rights
Police Brutality
Politicians and Ethics
Pollution
Prisons
Racism
Reproductive Technologies
The Rights of Animals
Sexual Harassment
Sexually Transmitted Diseases
Smoking
Suicide
Teen Addiction
Teen Pregnancy and Parenting
Teens and Alcohol
The Terrorist Attack on
    America
Urban Terrorism
Violence Against Women
Violence in the Media
Women in the Military